DREAM TO
REALISATION

The Business Owner's Journey

MATT MURPHY

National Library of Australia Cataloguing-in-Publication entry

Creator: Murphy, Matthew, author.

Title: Dream to Realisation—The Business Owner's Journey / Matthew Murphy

Book designed by Dedicated Book Services.

ISBN: 978-0-6481998-0-9 (paperback)

Subjects: Murphy, Matthew.
        Prime Financial (Listed Company)
        Accounting services—Australia.
        Superannuation—Australia.
        Finance, Personal—Australia.
        Assets (Accounting)—Australia.
        Tax planning—Australia.
        Estate planning—Australia.

Other Creators/Contributors: Dedicated Book Services, book designer.

Dream to Realisation—The Business Owner's Journey

Book Design by Dedicated Book Services

To my wife, Amanda, and our three children, Jack, Oscar and Abbey. You motivate me to be a better person every day.

Testimonials

It's funny, it's very practical and I need to follow the steps of each chapter. If I only do this, my business will be in far better shape at the end of this year than if I read 100 other business books.

Sarah McCrum
Coach and author of "Energy On Demand: master your personal energy and never burn out"
www.sarahmccrum.com

There are surprisingly few people on our planet who not only create great businesses but help others do that too. And they are even fewer who are Accountants! Matt's really an extraordinary business-builder. And this wonderful book is a rare case of something that does exactly what's promised in the title—it gives you everything you need to take your dreams to realisation. Better yet, Matt makes it a seriously enjoyable journey for you too.

Paul Dunn | Co-Founder and Chairman
B1G1® Simply stunning Business Giving

I've read many books on business. But this one is different. From choosing the right legal structure to simple but super effective growth strategies this book offers everything that the small business owner needs to build a successful business. And it's not theory. Matt is a successful entrepreneur in his own right as well as being an adviser to many successful business owners. So, what you get is implementable success tactics that have worked in the real world. My advice to any small business owner that aspires of achieving success is to read this book.

Marc Peskett
Partner
Prime Accounting and Business Advisory Pty Ltd

Business is tough and not getting any easier with the passage of time. By your side you need a mentor, coach, adviser and friend that understands and can share the journey with you. The pathway to success is rarely linear and this book by Matt Murphy is a how to guide to build in the layers required for sustainable growth and performance by getting down to the nub of WHY you do want you do. This publication combines Matt's years of experience advising some of this countries most successful entrepreneurs—if you are seeking success, this practical guide is a must read!

Simon Madder
Managing Director and CEO
Prime Financial Group

Contents

Foreword

The single most important lesson in this book is understanding the word WHY. Why is the key to business success. Knowing why you do something is an extremely powerful motivator. My Why is to inspire business owners to achieve the reason why they went into business in the first place. (My WHY is Your WHY.)

A deeper motivation for my Why is that I am personally inspired by the courage of business owners, as they have the guts to give it a go. I am also very grateful that I was born in Australia, a country that allows people to pursue their dreams and ambitions. Small and medium-size enterprises (SMEs) represent 47% of Australia's gross domestic product, and I want to help those driven and dedicated people make that number even larger. Small businesses employ 7 million Australians, accounting for 60% of the nation's workforce. To know that through my work and through this book I may play a tiny role in helping SMEs achieve success is hugely rewarding.

I believe that entrepreneurs' innovation-led businesses are the key for driving the Australian economy to ensure that our Lucky Country status remains.

From a selfish perspective, I needed to write this book. I had to get over twenty years of business knowledge out of my head. It had become pretty crowded in there, and I would like to create some more space to learn and teach new ideas.

The purpose of this book is to provide a real and practical map of what to do, and what not to do, when starting, operating and realising the value in your business. It is written from the perspective of real-life situations that textbooks and educational institutions do not prepare you for: the business school of hard knocks.

This book provides a guide as to how to turn the dream into a realisation. It explores and outlines the business owner's journey step-by-step, while addressing the mindset and emotional challenges that form part of the journey.

The secret to education is to make the complex simple through storytelling and providing everyday analogies. As such, this book is written using the analogy of a journey—taking a holiday road trip.

It is a summary of years of advice provided to business owners that took them from the dream of going into business to the realisation of that dream.

Writing this book has given me great pleasure, and I hope that you get what you need from it to realise your own dream.

Glossary

1PSP	One-Page Strategic Plan
ATO	Australian Taxation Office
BAS	Business Activity Statement
BHAG	Big Hairy Audacious Goal
CFO	Chief Financial Officer
CGT	Capital Gains Tax
CRM	Customer Relationship Management
EBM	Earning Based Method
EFT	Electronic Funds Transfer
EQ/EI	Emotional Intelligence
FME	Future Maintainable Earnings
GST	Goods and Services Tax
IPO	Initial Public Offering
KPI	Key Performance Indicator
NLP	Neuro-Linguistic Programming
PAYG	Pay As You Go
PSI	Personal Services Income
SME	Small Medium Enterprise
VAKD	Visual, Auditory, Kinesthetic and Digital
SMSF	Self-Managed Superannuation Fund
WIP	Work in Progress

Chapter 1

WHY ARE WE TRAVELLING ON THIS PATH?

The Ultimate Purpose

Before we start any journey, there must be a motivation. A motivation to achieve a result. The result could be as simple as driving to a destination. It is possible that people can start a journey unconsciously, but at some point in the journey, they will become conscious of achieving a desired outcome. Starting a business is just like any other journey. The people who focus right from the beginning are the ones who will actually make it to the destination and get there fast.

So how do we obtain focus on the journey? There is a simple one-word answer to this, and the answer is WHY. 'Why' is my favourite word in the English language. It disturbs us, it provides us clarity, it focuses us, and it provides motivation (which was captured well in Simon Sinek's book—*Start with Why*).

So why do people go into business in the first place? What drives people to go into business for themselves? After interviewing hundreds of business owners over the years as an advisor, I can tell you the answer. It is the dream. The dream of a better life. But what does 'a better life' mean? Often, business owners will question their choice to embark on their journey, wondering if their pursuit of the dream will indeed provide a better life and if that dream is even attainable.

People will start businesses to achieve the following objectives:

- Financial security and independence
- To satisfy a creative entrepreneurial flair
- Work/life balance
- The pursuit of excellence
- Control over one's destiny
- The creation of a legacy

Give this exercise a try. If you are currently in business, go back through the list above, and rate your personal feeling of achievement with respect to these categories from one to ten.

My next question to you is, if you didn't rate yourself an 8 or above in every category, then what are you going to do about it? Are you going to let your business dictate how you live your life, or are you going to take back control? Don't forget you went into business to have greater control over your destiny.

Most of the goals on that list resonate with people. Yet the last objective may require more explaining.

Achieving the first five objectives listed above is usually enough for most people. However, eventually many entrepreneurs find that those goals are not enough. Once they achieve the first five, they feel an ache. Or feel directionless. They know that there is a higher purpose driving them to achieve something greater than self. The first five points are self-centric—goals that define how you want to live your life with yourself, your friends and your family. But will you be satisfied to limit your scope to yourself and the people immediately around you? Or will you want to transform the lives of people around the world?

People who say 'Yes' to that last question are driven to create a difference for as many people as possible. To leave the planet a better place than when they arrived. They have a purpose greater than self. These people are visionaries—passionate people who have tapped into their Why. One of the most powerful lessons that I have learnt over the years is that if you connect with this, it permeates your business and will become your key to success. In everything—from sales to team alignment to personal happiness—knowing your Why will help you make the right calls, imagine creative solutions and give you the energy and the will to succeed when others fail.

Now that we have considered the dream, it's time to start the journey.

The Pre-Business Phase

Step One—The Why

Most students of business have learned that to create a business, you need to determine your vision and mission. The vision is what we want to achieve and the mission is how we are going to achieve it. Whilst the What and the How are important, the Why is the key to making it all happen.

VISION = What we want to achieve

MISSION = How we are going to get there

PURPOSE = Why we want to achieve it

You need to be clear on your Why before you start. Developing your purpose assists in articulating why you do what you do—not just for others but also for yourself. This will provide you with a strong focus. It answers the following questions that will be the foundations of your success:

Why do I get out of bed every day?

Why should someone buy my product or service?

Why should someone work as part of my business?

Why should suppliers support me?

Why should my family and friends support my journey and me?

The answers to these questions help to keep the mind focused on your intended outcome. This is hugely important once you are right in the thick of business and stuck in the process of day-to-day operations. It is at these times that most business owners start to lose their way and become disenchanted with the journey, resulting in making reactionary and usually poor decisions. By continually being focused on Why you went into business in the first place, you will have a greater chance of achieving the outcome you want and ultimately realising your dream.

We generally only see the success stories, but behind every success there is a frustration. From frustration comes creativity, and from creativity comes a breakthrough. If managed correctly, this breakthrough will result in achievement and success.

Think about it. Frustration arises because you are unable to solve a problem. This frustration can at times consume you. But unless the frustration exists, there will be no force to push you to solve the problem. Other issues will take up your time and consideration. On the other hand, if the frustration is not put into perspective, it can result once again in poor decision making. Your Why helps to provide that perspective. So knowing your Why is fundamental to succeeding in business throughout all its phases.

So, if you learn one thing from reading this book, discovering your Why is the most important one.

My Why is to inspire and lead business owners to achieve their Why. This is what gets me out of bed every day, why my customers choose me to help them and why my team works with me. (There has been discussion in public forums about the use of the word 'client' versus 'customer'. I will leave that discussion in the forums and will take the advice of Ron Baker and use the word 'customer' within this book.)

> **SUCCESS TIP**
> Develop your personal and business Why. Try to encapsulate your purpose for yourself and your business in one sentence. That done, your Why will enable you to keep the momentum in hard times. Have your Why close to you at all times to remind yourself of why you are doing what you are doing.

Step Two—The Law of Economics

Do you have a product or service that someone wants to buy? This fundamental question is another way of portraying the law of economics, Demand vs. Supply. There must be a need for your product or service. Without it there is no business. Some products and services are already required in the world, so history indicates that there is a need. But be careful, because history is not always the best indicator of the future. The world is currently experiencing a changing landscape driven by technology and globalisation (further suggested reading on this is a book by Thomas Friedman—*The World Is Flat*). And it's all changing at a faster pace than we've ever experienced before. This change may result in some products or supply sources going extinct. This is happening in businesses today—catching many entrepreneurs off guard. This effectively means that the business values in some industries are eroding as we speak.

Just think about the number of jobs in existence today that never existed thirty years ago. For all of those new industries that have sprouted up, businesses that were once prevalent have disappeared.

History has taught us that businesses can become defunct due to changes in the world. *Encyclopaedia Britannica* is one of the most significant examples. As a child growing up, the volumes of *Encyclopaedia Britannica* were the cornerstone of our learning and development. Many families had a set proudly sitting on their shelf or at minimum, each school had a set. It was the place to learn about the world. Think back thirty years. Could the directors of that organisation have possibly foreseen that their product was going to be rendered useless by technology? This is what happened to *Encyclopaedia Britannica*: Google and other search engines, combined with sites like Wikipedia, have now eliminated the need for a static book that goes out of date the day it is published. If this company had embraced technology and seen the warning signs earlier, they might still be in business today.

Many businesses will soon either be rendered useless or at best have their profit margins reduced. One example that is close to my heart is the accounting industry. If I project myself five years ahead, I believe that most compliance style accounting firms will be out of business or at best eroded in business value. This is largely due to technological advances and globalisation. We are already seeing advances in technology allowing information to be processed faster and more intuitively (consider what IBM is doing with *Watson*). The new generation of cloud-based accounting software simplifies the reporting process currently required by the majority of accounting software products. We are also seeing the jobs once completed by local employees going offshore to countries with cheaper labour forces.

This is just one example, in one part of one industry, yet it is happening everywhere.

So how do you keep your business alive? The trick is to get really creative with your thinking and ask yourself three questions:

- Will there still be a market for the product or service that I am selling in the future?
- Could technology or globalisation replace what I can do?
- How can I pivot ahead of the change?

When there isn't a future for certain businesses, we call those businesses 'sunset industries'.

So what is needed is to ensure that your business will be as relevant—if not more relevant—in the future or that it can be adapted as the world evolves (further suggested reading on this is the book by Clayton Christensen—*The Innovator's Dilemma*).

Jack Welch has suggested that if you foresee that the speed of change outside your business is greater than the speed of change possible from the inside, then you need to innovate ('pivot') and change your business model and product/service, otherwise the end is near.

SUCCESS TIP
Think innovatively. What will the next five years look like for your products and business industry?

Step Three—Is the Business Idea Scalable?

Before you can go into business, you must have an idea that can be turned into a product or service that someone wants to buy. If someone wants to buy your product or service, then you have a business. The mistake that some people make is in overlooking the fact that some business ideas are scalable and can grow into a much larger business while others only present an income stream for the owner. A popular term of phrase for an income stream is 'buying yourself a job'. A lot of service-based franchises are designed for just that reason.

So you need to consider what the business can possibly achieve. What is the best possible outcome for all of your hard work? Is it possible to scale this business or does it rely purely on personal effort alone? This is more of an issue for service-based businesses than product-based businesses. There is nothing wrong with an income stream that satisfies some of the objectives. The underlying issue is that people have greater expectations than the business model can provide.

Moreover, there are many business models that can be scalable to a certain size but need to evolve fundamentally to grow beyond a certain point. An example of this is a graphic design business. These businesses generally can scale to between ten and twenty employees. The cornerstone of the success of these businesses is the creativity of the leaders and staff in the company. But creativity comes from the individual and is therefore hard to productise. Sure, there are examples where businesses have been successful in scaling above this size, but it will require a huge amount of leadership to align the creativity of the team to ensure consistency across the business. These businesses are very much in the minority; the majority will max out at fewer than twenty employees.

Now nothing's wrong with having a business that has ten to twenty employees. The point is that this is the norm, so if you are considering going into business or are in a very individual labour-focused business, be sure that you know your limitations. This will reduce the frustration of trying to achieve something that is difficult to achieve. It also dictates the succession plan exit options for the business, which we will discuss later in the book. Other books that discuss scale are Verne Harnish's books titled *Mastering the Rockefeller Habits: What You Must Do to Increase the Value of Your Growing Firm* and, more recently, *Scaling Up.*

Step Four—Mindset. Do You Have What It Takes?

Once you have established that there is a product or service that has a demand which can be generated into a business and not just an income stream based on one's personal efforts alone, it is now important to assess your capabilities in taking that dream into the realisation phase. You need to consider what is possible for this business and whether you are the person who has the ability to make it happen.

Starting and running a business is not for the faint-hearted. It takes courage and effort to build a business and realise the dream. Failure occurs for a number of reasons, one of which is due to the mental strength and discipline of the business owner. I have never met a business owner who hasn't lain awake at night worrying if they can pay the wages of their team or that they may have to let employees go if the next day's sales meeting doesn't go their way.

The journey is tough but hugely rewarding. It provides a platform of creativity and satisfaction beyond most life journeys because if you get it right, then you can achieve the reason Why you went into business in the first place, which can create amazing satisfaction. Pushing through frustration and challenge to achieve your goals is an exhilarating feeling. It provides some wonderful highs but also some horrible lows. The trick is to manage both well and remain focused on your Why. Discipline is the key to staying on track. (Brian Tracy provides some great tips for staying on track with his book *Eat that Frog! 21 Great Ways to Stop Procrastinating and Get More Done in Less Time.*)

Physically acting in a disciplined way is no guarantee of having a disciplined mind. You can get up every day at 5 a.m., exercise before work and work productively all day, achieving everything your business requires to be successful. But if you have an undisciplined mind, you will lie awake at night worrying about the 'what ifs'.

You may be physically present at home with your family and friends, but not mentally present and engaged in your relationships. If you are able to control the mind and focus your energy, then you will live a more enjoyable life along the journey and have a better chance of seeing it through to the end to realise your goals and aspirations. (Further reading in these areas is suggested by authors such as Tony Robbins, Eckhart Tolle, Sarah McCrum, Jack Canfield and Stephen Covey.)

You know yourself better than anyone; you know your strengths and weaknesses. You need to assess yourself against the demands of a business owner. Do you have the mental discipline to cope with the difficulties of owning and operating a business? My advice is if not, don't do it. Or if not and you are still inspired by the idea of being in business and what it has to offer, then learn how to focus.

One way to focus your mind is to learn the tools of mind focus. There are lots of books written on this topic and lots of experts available who are trained either medically or spiritually to assist. My belief is that just like most people need a personal trainer to stay fit, high-performing people need a mindset coach to help them remain focused. I understand that for some people there is a stigma against going to a psychologist, psychiatrist or other mind coaches. It may be seen as a weakness. I encourage you all to fight this social stigma and engage a professional to assist you with the journey. They will help you remain focused and ensure that the important areas of your life will not suffer.

It's all about staying realistically positive. (Martin Seligman discusses more ideas around this in his books *Learned Optimism* and *Authentic Happiness: Using the New Positive Psychology to Realize Your Potential for Lasting Fulfillment*.) This may seem a bit of a contradictory statement, but what this actually means is that you need to make sure that negativity does not creep into your thinking. You need to remain positive; however, you need to make sure that the positivity is not blind. By facing and answering your 'what ifs' you will remain realistic, and you will be able to use your fears as fuel to help your business grow. A lot of the 'what ifs' are negative, and if they occur, they will have a negative impact on your business. If you let your mind believe that these failures will inevitably happen, you will lie awake at night worrying. But if you are able to prepare for the 'what if' scenarios so you have them covered if they occur—while remaining in a positive state of mind that it will work out for the best—you have a formula for success.

SUCCESS TIP
Remain positively realistic.

If you have read to the end of this chapter and decided that business is for you, keep reading. Now you can get into the nitty gritty of business and how to create a framework that is more likely to see you have success in navigating your dream to realisation.

Chapter 2

WHERE ARE
WE GOING?

Vision, Strategy, Accountability

Often, I use an analogy when explaining the business vernacular of Vision, Strategy and Accountability. The analogy is travel. The vision is the destination, the strategy is the map and the road signs are the financial information, which keeps you on track.

Let's look at each one of these in turn.

1. VISION

What is your destination? Or as Stephen Covey notes in his book *The 7 Habits of Highly Effective People* – Begin with the end in mind.

Your vision is what you want to achieve. What is the ultimate goal of the business? If you have been a student of business, you may have read a lot about how to create a vision. My formula for creating a vision is slightly different from most. The concept is the same, but the method is different.

Beyond the 'why', the Vision also should incorporate the 'what', 'to whom' and 'where'.

Your Vision should as be genuine as your Why. I recommend that you test your vision by verbalising it to your family, friends, trusted colleagues and anyone who will listen. Whilst it is great to get feedback, and I always recommend seeking it, often the best test for any of the concepts that I teach is to verbalise. When it comes out of your mouth you will become your own critic, and you will know whether that vision is genuine or not. Genuineness is the key. If you believe it, then there is a greater chance that others will too. You may have heard the word 'passion'. Passion is the result of belief. So believe, and you will be passionate about what you do. Passion creates a following and will result in momentum. Momentum is required for success.

The more articulate you are about your Vision and purpose, the more likely people will be to engage with it and want to be a part of it. The more support you have, the greater the chance will be that you will arrive at your destination.

So it becomes a self-fulfilling prophecy.

> **SUCCESS TIP**
> Verbalise your vision to as many people as you can in order to establish its genuineness. You will not need others to provide you feedback on the Vision statement itself. But if you genuinely believe in it, this will be evident, and the people around you will be more likely to believe in it too.

2. STRATEGY

Once the destination has been determined, we need to work out how to get there. Strategy is the plan.

Before you start to strategise, you need to complete an exercise of self-reflection. Are you a person who likes or dislikes detail? Some people are naturally big picture oriented and some prefer the detail. If you are unsure what you are, I suggest that you complete a personality profile. One of my favourite personality profiles is DISC (more on that in Chapter 8).

We will discuss the importance of self-reflection and self-awareness in later chapters of this book. The reason I am raising it at this point is that a lot of people stumble at the planning stage—either by over- or under-analysing everything. Both extremes are detrimental.

If you are big picture person, you're more likely to want to get going and hope that it will all fall into place. My observations of these people are that they are generally optimistic in their outlook and back their judgements. As indicated in Chapter 1, a positive attitude is a fantastic attribute to have—but you need to temper that with being realistically positive. Part of that realism is about planning well. If you are not known to pay attention to details, plan. You can never do enough planning because, as the saying goes, 'The devil is in the details'.

If you are a detailed person, you are more likely to have a pessimistic outlook and want to plan for every contingency possible. Whilst this is a tremendous trait to have, it can be the reason why so many businesses either never start or never progress to their full potential. They often let *perfect* get in the way of *better*. Sheryl Sandberg and Guy Kawasaki have made reference to this ideal with references like 'Done is better than perfect' and 'Don't worry, be crappy.' Both of these quotes are around simply getting the idea out to the market so it can be tested and then work out what needs to be adjusted.

Understanding this concept is extremely important, as it will stop you from under- or over-analysing, which can keep your business from progressing or might cause it to fail due to simply not shipping on any ideas that you have, while you analyse the risks.

So what is strategy? Strategy is the direction in which you need to travel in order to arrive at your destination.

How do you strategise? The best framework I have come across for strategising is to focus on the four distinct areas of business:

- Marketing
- Sales
- Delivering
- Servicing (Post Sales)

Carefully considering all four areas will help you turn a prospect into a customer and from a customer into a raving fan. A raving fan for your business is the ultimate goal, as this will generate new business without incurring further marketing costs. (Consider reading Amanda Stevens' book *Turning Customers into Advocates*.)

We will explore each of these areas in the book.

My philosophy is always to plan with the end in mind. Or plan to im- plement. Every plan should have an implementation strategy. So many times I see business owners plan but never execute. They write 100-page business plans that sit on the shelf and gather dust. Therefore they fail to implement. Failure to implement is another key reason businesses collapse.

I have run many business planning and strategic planning sessions with business owners. Often I hear the comment, 'We know what we have to do.' This is true; there are no new business concepts. Because of this, my focus with my customers is on implementing their own strategies. All of the business tools I use are implementation-oriented. One of the best implementation business tools that I use is the One-Page Strategic Plan (1PSP) that has been developed by Verne Harnish from Gazelles Corp. Inc. This plan is based on John D. Rockefeller's 'habits for success', and more than anything, it teaches you how to implement your plans (as detailed in Harnish's book—*Mastering the Rockefeller Habits*).

In business we get caught up in the day-to-day operational issues, which can often mean that we lose sight of the big picture. The big picture is the thing that keeps us motivated and the reason why we get out of bed. The 1PSP provides you with the ability to see your big picture goals combined with your detailed action plan. Having that written summary will help you to always remember why you are in business and what your ultimate objective is. It becomes the conduit between the big picture and the daily tasks.

So whether you are a big picture person or a detail-oriented person, this tool will assist you in focusing on the things that you do not naturally focus on. It balances out both types of people by providing the discipline for each personality style.

SUCCESS TIP
Don't get caught up on completing a business plan; change your focus and prepare a business implementation plan.

3. ACCOUNTABILITY

Why do large businesses generally succeed whilst small businesses fail? Many of us will have heard the statistic "75% of small businesses fail within the first five years of operation." This is not because there isn't a demand for the product. It is due to the lack of infrastructure and discipline. A large part of discipline is accountability. I have spent the best part of twenty years holding business owners accountable to their plans—not because they lack the ability to keep themselves accountable, but because they lack the discipline.

For a large business to survive, the right levels of accountability must be in place. Internally, organisations are hierarchically structured. This is also generally true for a small business. However, in a large business the directors hold the CEO accountable, and the chairman keeps the board of directors accountable. It is the board's responsibility to act on behalf of the shareholders and make all decisions for the best interests of the shareholders.

By contrast, the small business owner has to wear multiple hats. They are usually the CEO, the director, the chairman and the shareholder, all rolled into one. This is largely where things go pear-shaped. It is not effective, efficient or productive for any person to exercise a diverse range of skill sets, all the while expending the time and mental discipline to continually keep themselves accountable to themselves. It is extremely difficult to have clear thoughts to make decisions and obtain perspective when you are working in the business.

Some business owners intuitively understand this issue and reach out for assistance, whilst others wait for this deficiency in their model to be pointed out. The best way to correct this deficiency is to start thinking and acting like a large business.

Start by having monthly meetings and invite a trusted advisor. These meetings do not have to be as formal and stuffy as we might imagine board meetings to be. They can be as informal as you like, as long as you cover off on the relevant information to be able to make informed decisions. I have spent plenty of time in pubs, cafes and restaurants with business owners on a monthly basis, discussing and making decisions about their business. I go wherever the owner is most comfortable. Sometimes I insist that the meetings be held in a boardroom, if I know that the business owner is easily distracted in their place of work.

A monthly meeting requires you to get out of the day-to-day operational mode of thinking to start to think more strategically about your business. The old adage of working 'on' rather than 'in' your business is as relevant today as it has been for centuries.

I will discuss the contents, the information to be reviewed and the decisions to be made by the business owner later in this book. The main point to get across now is the importance of building the necessary infrastructure and discipline in your business. In any way you can, try to recreate the infrastructure and the accountability of a large business in your company as the business owner.

Who is keeping you accountable to your plan? If you are not doing a good job, then find someone who can. When selecting the right people to hold yourself accountable, you need to consider the following:

- Do I respect this person and consider what he or she has to say, even if we don't agree?

- Do I trust that this person has the best interests of the business, and ultimately my best interests at heart?

- Does this person have the skill set that I do not have, to balance up my deficiencies?

It is important to surround yourself with people who have the same values as you but think differently. All too many times I see people select mentors, coaches, chairs of boards and advisors that think the same as they do. They select these people because, generally, they will agree on everything. Life is a lot easier and has less conflict when the people around you agree with you. We are wired in a fashion to gravitate towards people who are like us. Therefore it takes a strong will to succeed to engage a person that you disagree with, especially when you are paying this person.

If you select the right person or persons, this can be the difference between success or mediocrity or worse—failure.

> **SUCCESS TIP**
> Implement monthly board meetings. Invite advisors who share your values, but think differently.

To get something, you need to give something up. That will usually be time or money or both.

Chapter 3

ARE WE ACTUALLY GOING TO START THIS JOURNEY?

Business Structures

It's time to make it real. Creating a business structure is like giving birth to the idea. It brings the business idea into a physical being. As a student of business, I know that business structures can be difficult to understand. Nevertheless, I am still astounded that most business owners I come across—even ones who have been in business for years—do not understand their structure and how it works. I do not place all of the blame on the business owner; the accountant also shares responsibility. Whilst I am an accountant/business advisor and love my profession, it is disappointing to learn that some of my colleagues do not educate and support their customers to the level that they should. If you fall into this category, do yourself a favour and go find another accountant. Why should business owners keep their business with an accountant/advisor who does merely an okay job? For most business owners, their company is their biggest asset, so trusting it to a person just because you like them is not appropriate.

SUCCESS TIP
Business success is about implementation, so get off your backside and go source the best advisors you can.

Discussing this topic in a book is very dangerous for you, the reader. I do not recommend that you operate heavy machinery whilst doing so just in case you fall asleep. If you do suffer from insomnia, then I can recommend that you read this chapter for a quick remedy. If you are a parent, another benefit of this chapter is to use it as a bedtime story for your kids. Even if you use funny voices, they will quickly fall asleep. This subject is best explained in person using a white board. But in the absence of you and I getting together, I thought I'd make this as painless as possible for us both by summarising the essential ideas you must know.

One further disclaimer, nothing in this chapter amounts to advice. It is necessarily general in nature. You should not take action, or decide against taking action, based on anything in this chapter. Rather, any decisions should be made as a result of specific specialist advice based on your exact situation. Warnings along these lines will be repeated throughout this chapter.

In structuring a business, there is no 'one size fits all'. In order to determine the most appropriate structure for your business, you need to go through a process. The process involves stepping through the following key areas:

- Asset Protection
- Profit Distribution (and tax planning)
- Equity and Finance
- Succession Planning

There are multiple structures to choose from that may be appropriate to select for your business.

The main structures that are available to be used for running a business are:

- Company
- Unit Trust
- Partnership of Trusts
- Discretionary (Family) Trusts
- Partnerships
- Sole Trader
- A combination of all of the above

In order to determine which of the above structures is appropriate, we need to discuss each of the key areas listed above for each structure.

Asset Protection

Why is asset protection important when you own a business? Owning and operating a SME is a risky business. (Great name for a movie!) There is a lot that can and does go wrong. So the purpose of asset protection in a business is to minimise the downside whilst maximising the upside.

So what does asset protection actually mean? For most people, it is not losing their house if everything goes pear-shaped in the business. From my perspective, it is all about the segregation of assets to ensure that one asset is not affected by another asset. This all has to do with legal entities and creating siloes.

Many people also consider the protection of wealth on personal relationship breakdown as a key aspect of asset protection. This issue is an entire book in itself and outside the scope of this book.

In your journey throughout life, you will accumulate wealth through the purchase of assets. Those assets usually fall into the following broad categories:

- Home
- Investment Property
- Investment Portfolio (shares and managed investments)
- Business
- Superannuation
- Lifestyle Assets (holiday house, cars, boats, etc.)

Each one of these assets has an appropriate owner to ensure that the appropriate level of asset protection is achieved. All asset classes listed above are deemed what we generally call passive investments, except for a business. A business is classed as an active asset. The risk of being sued whilst owning passive assets is comparatively lower, so the risk of affecting other assets because of their demise is low; whereas the risk of being held responsible for the trading of a business is significantly higher due to the varied risks of running a business.

So asset protection is generally not as big an issue for people holding passive assets alone; it really only becomes an issue when a business is involved.

This being said, to say that there are no asset protection issues for individuals that are not operating a business is incorrect; it is just significantly reduced. Taking out insurance can reduce the risks that exist against the loss of these assets. Moreover, while I've noted that people don't consider themselves as an asset, in a commercial sense this is what they are. For most people, they themselves are their biggest asset because they will earn a significant amount of money over their lifetime through employment and investment. If you consider yourself as an investment asset and start to treat yourself as one, there is a greater chance that you will protect what you accumulate. Like any asset, to protect it, you should insure it. There are two ways of doing this: protecting your earning capacity and protecting others from the damage that you can potentially cause.

Consider it like a car. Full comprehensive car insurance does two things: it protects the owner from having to pay for the damage he might cause to another car and the damage caused to their own car. If we use this analogy for a person, you should have two levels of insurance—insurance against the damage that you might cause to yourself and to others.

Following is a list of insurances that relate to the damage that you cause to yourself:

- Income Protection
- Trauma
- Life Insurance
- Temporary and Permanent Disability
- Health Insurance

The insurance is there to provide you with an income or payment to cover loss of earnings or for compensation for loss. Ultimately, these insurances are there to provide you with protection for you and your family's lifestyle at a time of sickness or death.

The following is a list of insurances that relate to the damage that you can potentially cause to others:

- Public Liability Insurance

- Car Insurance

- Sports Insurance (such as golfer's insurance)

- Transport Accident Commission (TAC)–(part of car registration)

- Professional Indemnity Insurance

The insurance is there to protect you from having to pay for the damage caused to others. Golfer's insurance is one that I have only recently been made aware of. Most golfers will be covered for this insurance if they are members of a course or organisation that includes it in the membership. However, the average social golfer without a handicap is not covered for damage she might cause to others on the golf course. There have been court cases where an injured person has successfully sued for damages caused by a golf ball striking the claimant's head causing brain damage. So the next time you are standing on the fourth tee with slow-playing golfers in front of you and you want to give them the hurry along by driving a ball close to them, think again!

If you have read this far into this chapter, well done. I know that it can be a bit depressing and morbid discussing insurance, but I am amazed at the number of people who are underinsured. To ensure that I protect myself, I must again note that none of the above constitutes advice to the reader in any way. As mentioned near the start of this chapter, I recommend that you speak to your personal financial advisor with respect to the protection of your assets.

Now we turn our attention to the risks associated with running a business. About ten years ago, I heard a statistic indicating that Sydney, Australia, had become the most litigious city per capita in the world, even surpassing Los Angeles. Even if this statistic weren't entirely true, it wouldn't surprise me if it were close. Given that thought, it is clear we live in a world of risk. Business owners face risk every day and this is another reason why I believe they are courageous.

Now, choosing certain business entities exposes the business owner to higher levels of personal risk than others. So again, the trick with effective business structuring is to protect your personal and investment assets away from your business assets.

Let's review the effectiveness of each of the main structures from an asset protection perspective.

Sole Trader

Being a sole trader means you are operating the business in your own name. Based on my experience, I have found that some people can get confused with this concept. This is due to the fact they will apply to the Office of Fair Trading to obtain a trading or business name. They sometimes think that the name becomes a separate entity from them. To be very clear, the legal owner of the name is the person liable for every aspect of their business.

There is an inability to protect any assets directly owned by the sole trader from liabilities incurred by the operations of their business. If they are held liable for their actions in business, and they are unable to pay for the damages arising from the action (having claimed any available insurance), then their personal assets are at risk of being used to pay for the damages. Bankruptcy is used as the mechanism by which your personal assets are exposed to payment of your business liabilities.

The benefit of a sole trader structure is that it is cheap to set up and cheap to administer; however, it can be dangerous from an asset protection perspective. To protect yourself, make sure that you limit the assets in your name and have sufficient business insurance policies in place that will protect you against potential liabilities arising from loss or damage.

Partnerships

A partnership is the coming together of two or more parties, whether it is individuals or entities, to form a relationship. This relationship is usually connected by an asset like property ownership or business assets. Partnerships can be formed by individuals, companies or trusts. There are also a variety of partnership forms, including general partnerships, limited partnerships and corporate partnerships. The most common form of partnership for SMEs is a general partnership. In this type of partnership, it is important to understand that it is not a legal entity. Rather, each partnership asset is owned by the partners of the partnership in the agreed percentages.

From an asset protection point of view, the partners are the legal entities and therefore will each be responsible for the liabilities of the business. Whilst the partners will enjoy the benefits of the income and capital based on agreed proportions, they are jointly and severally liable. What does jointly and severally liable actually mean? It means that the person owed money does not have to recover the money from the partners in their partnership proportions. Therefore if one partner has more assets than the other, the partner may have a greater liability (including up to 100% of the claim) to repay the money owed.

One way to avoid this inequity between partners is for each individual to set up their own new company or trust structure and only have assets of the partnership in these entities. If the partners in a partnership are individuals, the assets in their own names will be exposed to the liabilities of the partnership just like a sole trader, with the added exposure of joint and several liabilities.

Company

Before we discuss the asset protection characteristics of a company, it is probably worth giving you a lesson on what a company is. (I promise to make this as quick and painless as possible.) As a starting point, the most important thing to remember is that a company is a legal person. It is created and has a life. The main point to note about this is as a 'person', it is liable for its actions and can be sued.

Here's a quick story just to keep you awake. You know the lane on freeways that is designated for multiple passengers, the transit lane? Well, one day a person was driving down the transit lane with just the driver in the car. The police pulled the car over to question the driver as to why he was using the transit lane without a passenger and to issue him a fine. The driver responded by saying that he had a passenger next to him in the car and pointed to his company folder with the common seal. (The common seal was a stamp made which effectively became the company's signature. Now it's not required to be used.) The officer was not amused and issued the fine. I'm not sure if this ticket was contested—and the whole story may be one of those urban myths—but I thought it was a good one.

Anyway, back to the topic of what is a company. A company has the following relationships. It has director(s) and shareholder(s). The shareholder is the owner of the company and she delegates her authority to the directors to operate the business. The director's responsibility is to operate the business for the benefit of the shareholders. There are different types of companies:

- Public companies listed on the stock exchange
- Public companies not listed on the stock exchange
- Companies limited by guarantee

- Large proprietary (private) companies

- Proprietary (private) companies

The most common company structure used for SME entities is a proprietary (private) company. A proprietary (private) company has the reference 'Pty Ltd' at the end of its name. 'Pty' stands for proprietary and 'Ltd' stands for limited.

In most small companies, the shareholders and directors are usually one and the same; however, where they are not, then the directors must be very conscious of acting in the best interests of the shareholders.

One of the best benefits of a company is that it has good limited liability characteristics. The company is liable for its actions. Whilst the actions are driven by the directors and employees of the company, it is all on behalf of the company. Shareholders are not required to contribute to the debts of the company, thus their liability is limited to the funds invested into the company. This is commonly referred to as the corporate veil. However, there are certain circumstances where the directors can be held responsible for the debts of the company.

If a director is held responsible for the debts of the company, his personal assets may be exposed. The following is a non-exhaustive list of the main types of situations where a director can be held responsible for the debts of the company:

Insolvency Trading
If the director continues to trade the business when there is an inability for the company to pay its debts as and when they fall due, the director can be held personally liable for those debts.

Tax Liabilities
Directors can be held personally liable for the tax withheld from the wages of employees and for the unpaid superannuation contributions of their employees.

Fraud

Directors can be personally responsible for fraudulent activities.

Guarantees

If a director has given a personal guarantee on behalf of the company, they are personally liable if the company defaults on the repayment of the liability.

Legislation Breaches

In certain circumstances directors can be personally held responsible for legislation breaches, for example, under workplace health and safety laws.

SUCCESS TIP

If you are going to become a director of a company, limit the personal and investment assets you have in your name. If you have a spouse that is not at risk, you could plan to put your family home in his or her name. If you have significant personal or investment assets, either put them in the name of your spouse or set up a discretionary family trust. (We will discuss the benefits of a trust further in this chapter.)

The purpose of this strategy is that in the event you are exposed as a director and you are forced to pay the debts of the company, you are protecting your family assets to ensure that you do not lose the lot in an action against the company. This is because it is only the assets in your personal name that are at risk. Now for some of you, this may seem unethical or immoral; however, sometimes directors can be held responsible for things that are outside of their control. We are not advocating that they walk away from their responsibilities, but we do want to protect them from unfair losses arising from things that can be outside their control. I have witnessed multiple situations where business owners have been sued unfairly by customers and employees, and the legal system has failed to protect them.

The asset protection issue that most business owners and their accountant/advisors fail to recognise is that if the shareholding is in the same name as the director's, then this asset is exposed in the event that the director is responsible for the debts of the company. A possible way to avoid this is, once again, for the spouse or a discretionary family trust to own the shares.

This will ensure that you have asset protection from a company and personal perspective.

SUCCESS TIP
Ensure that, where possible, the directors do not hold the shares in the company in their own name. The shares should be owned by the spouse or a discretionary family trust.

Discretionary Family Trust

So what is a trust? There are multiple types of trusts, with the most prevalent ones being:

- Discretionary (Family) Trust
- Unit (Fixed) Trusts
- Hybrid Trusts
- Self-Managed Superannuation Funds

They all have a set of common and unique characteristics.

Once again, before we get into the asset protection characteristics of a trust, let me present to you Trusts 101 (with the repeated disclaimer, this is only a very general overview). There are multiple relationships in a trust:

Appointor

The appointor has the most control of the trust because one of its main functions is to add, change or remove the trustee. Importantly, not all trusts have this role and those that do may use other names such as principal, guardian or nominator.

Trustee

Pending removal by the appointor, the trustee is responsible for administering the trust day-to-day, based on the rules outlined in the trust deed. The trustee manages the assets on behalf of the beneficiaries, and in a family trust, has the power to distribute the income and the capital of the trust to eligible beneficiaries at its complete discretion.

Settlor

The settlor contributes the first asset to create the trust. This is an extremely important point that most people who have trusts don't really understand. A trust is created by an asset. The whole purpose of a trust is for an asset to be held and controlled for the benefit of a beneficiary. The asset that is contributed to form the trust must be protected and remain intact. If this asset is no longer held by the trust, the trust potentially dissolves. It is also important to ensure that the settlor cannot benefit from the income or assets of the trust.

Beneficiaries

The beneficiaries are the individuals or entities to which the assets are to be held for the benefit of. In a discretionary trust, there are normally specified (or named) and general (or unnamed) beneficiaries. Specified or primary beneficiaries are the individuals that are the nucleus of the trust beneficiaries. The general class of beneficiaries are the family members of the beneficiaries.

Trusts were first created back in the 1600s when individuals were going off to war. These people requested their close friends to look after their assets for their family. Effectively, these friends, now known as trustees, would have to control, protect and administer the assets based on the wishes of their friends who contributed the assets of the trust for the benefit of their family.

A discretionary family trust is a vehicle that affords high levels of asset protection. This is because the beneficiaries do not have an indefeasible right to the assets of the trust, as it is up to the discretion of the trustee as to who is entitled to the income and capital of the trust. Therefore, the assets of the trust do not form part of the assets of any individual beneficiary. So if we think of a situation where an individual is liable for damages created from her business, whether as a director or directly as a sole trader, the assets of the trust are not exposed to assisting with the discharge of the liability.

If the trust operates a business, then the assets of the trust are exposed to liabilities created by the trust. The trustee is required to discharge the obligation to pay the liabilities, but only to the level of assets held in the trust and those of the trustee. There is no obligation for the beneficiaries or settlor to contribute to the trust where there is a short-fall. Legally, there can be an obligation for the trustee to pay for the liabilities of the trust where the assets of the trust are unable to cover the payment of the liabilities. To provide an extra level of protection, it is recommended that a company be incorporated to act as the trustee of the trust. The value of the company should only be nominal (for example $2). This means, even though the trustee is potentially liable for the debts of the trust, no financial detriment is incurred. Generally the individual who was otherwise proposed as the trustee will become the director and shareholder of the trustee company to ensure that she has control over the trust.

A further point to note with appointors: there is a potential risk con-cerning the appointor. If the appointor becomes bankrupt, there have been court cases where the trustee in bankruptcy has attempted to replace the appointor. Upon replacement of the appointor, the trustee in bankruptcy would then replace the trustee of the trust with themselves and distribute the income and the capital to the bankrupt beneficiary, to pay out the bankrupt creditors. While no trustee in bankruptcy has been successful in this approach to date, it is generally seen as appropriate to have more than one appointor, which may include an independent person that is not a beneficiary of the trust.

> **SUCCESS TIP**
> For increased asset protection, ensure that the trustee is a company (with paid up capital of $2) for a trading business trust. Also consider having multiple appointors, which may include an independent person.

Unit Trusts

Unit trusts are fundamentally the same as discretionary trusts, except for one point: the trustee no longer has discretion as to who is entitled to the income and capital of the trust. The distribution from a trust will be fixed based on the units owned in the trust. It essentially works in the same way as a company with regards to shares. Based on the number of units you have in the unit trust, you will be entitled to the proportion of income and capital of the trust.

If structured correctly, a unit trust has the same level of protection as a company with respect to ownership of shares in that the units form part of the owner's assets but the unit holders should not be liable for the activities of the trust. Therefore, the units are another asset, which can be exposed to the liabilities of the owner.

Hybrid Trusts

A hybrid trust is a combination of a discretionary trust and a Unit (Fixed) Trust. Whilst there are unit holders of the trust and therefore a notional fixed entitlement to the income and capital of the trust, the trustee also has discretionary powers to distribute income and capital outside the fixed entitlement proportions.

Hybrid trusts can be particularly complex to implement and have historically been the subject of attention from the Tax Office.

Self-Managed Super Funds

A self-managed superannuation fund (SMSF) is a special form of trust set up solely for the purpose of funding retirement. There are many regulatory restrictions on what an SMSF can do. One of the restrictions is that from the Tax Office's perspective it generally should not operate a business. As it has this restriction, we will not be covering off on the use of this type of structure, other than to say that an SMSF should be considered as a part of structuring strategy for business owners, particularly because assets in superannuation (including an SMSF) are generally completely safe from attack.

Profit Distribution

Considering profit distribution is important for two reasons:

- Ensuring the appropriate persons get the appropriate profit of the business
- Minimisation of tax

Before we get into the nitty-gritty of how this works, I thought that I would share an insight to my world.

I would love to have a dollar for every Monday morning phone call I receive from customers and friends who say that they were at a barbecue yesterday, and this guy they were speaking to doesn't pay any tax because of how he is structured. Before I provide you my answer, there's one observation I would like to make: it is always a guy and not a girl talking, and it is always at a barbecue. The picture I have in mind is 'a bloke with a beer in one hand, Bar-B-Mate in the other, and speaking with authority on a subject that he knows little about.' We have all been guilty of this at barbecues. However, it would be nice not to receive these calls on a Monday because of the Bar-B-Mate expert from the weekend. My response to customers is usually the same: 'Our advice has not changed, regardless of the hot tip from Mr. Bar-B-Mate.' (Note to self: I wonder if all professionals have to deal with the same Monday morning call.)

Whenever Monday morning rolls around and I get this call again, here's what I'm always tempted to say, 'Please, tell your friend to give me his number, as he clearly knows more about structuring and tax than I do. It seems that my two decades of experience as a tax advisor has been wasted.' However, my usual response is, 'That's great. Did he happen to provide the specific details? Do you think he is being legitimate and getting the right advice? Maybe I should have a quick chat with him?'

Here's the thing. Yes, there are many ways to minimise your tax. There are even ways to not pay any tax, but every situation is different, and each situation must be taken on its own merits. I have helped customers successfully and legitimately pay minimal tax (and in some cases no tax) on transactions using the law as it is intended. However, I do have a moral stance on the payment of tax. If you want to live in a magnificent country such as Australia, then you should pay for the privilege. If you use the infrastructure of roads, hospitals, education, etc., then you should pay for their use. When prospective customers meet with me and advise that they do not wish to pay any tax at all, ever, I tell them that I'm not an accountant who can help with that.

It is my job to advise customers on paying the right amount of tax. The right amount is the minimum amount based on the correct application of the applicable laws. I love saving people tax expenditures, but it is never at the detriment of performance. It is interesting that some people say, 'I do not want to earn any more money because it is not worth it. I'll have to pay more in taxes.' Whilst this is true in part, for every extra dollar of money you earn, yes, you pay tax, but you are still better off, as you have more money in your pocket. The highest rate of tax in Australia is 45% at present (excluding Medicare). This means that for every dollar you earn, even if you are paying tax at the highest tax rate, you are still pocketing over 50 cents. So, if you have the ability to earn more, don't let taxes deter you. You'll still be better off.

Now that I have got that off my chest, let's talk about a topic close to everyone's heart, tax minimisation. Following the approach of the asset protection section, I will cover each structure, how profits are distributed and how much tax will be payable. Note that I will only mention tax minimisation, which is legal. Tax avoidance is illegal and can result in fines, penalties, interest and in some cases, incarceration. Tax avoidance is something I avoid in my business and it is avoided in this book.

Sole Trader

As we already covered, a sole trader operates his business in his own name. Any profit that he generates from his business will be added to any other income that he generates from employment or investments. Tax is then payable by the person on all income earned at the individual marginal tax rates. My experience indicates that most people are fine with paying up to 30% of their income in tax but have difficulty paying above this amount. The problem with this is, that once an individual earns over $87,000, the tax rate increases beyond 30%, and once an individual earns over $180,000, the tax rate increases to close to 50% once government levies (for example the Medicare levy of up to 2.5%) are added.

Partnership

The profits of a partnership are distributed to the partners in proportion to their equity interest in the partnership. A general partnership is not a legal entity, and is not considered an entity that is liable for income tax. As such, the individual partners are responsible for the tax on the profits of their portion of the partnership. Subsequently, the tax they will pay will depend on the structure of each individual partner. For example, this could be an individual, a trust or a company.

Company

A company, by law, is considered a natural, legal person and as such is a taxable entity; this means it will pay taxes in its own right. A company currently pays a flat tax rate of 30% on its taxable profit, although in some situations the rate can be 27%. This seems to trigger a psychological effect, because customers find paying 30% of their income in tax much more palatable. Practically speaking, the benefit of a company rather than a partnership or a trust is that the company is responsible for payment of its own tax. So the 70% left over can be used to invest back in the business or to pay a dividend to shareholders. There are no requirements for loans or further capital injections from the partners of a partnership or beneficiaries after they have received their profit distributions and paid their own tax, which can be at different rates.

From experience, the most concerning issue for under-advised business owners is that they believe that the profit of the company can be applied for personal use. When this practice starts, it is a very slippery slope to dire consequences and in some cases, bankruptcy.

Let me explain. There are only four ways that you can take money out of a company for the personal use of the owners:

1. Salary and Wages
2. Dividends
3. Return of Capital
4. Loan

The first three ways do not cause future problems due to the transaction triggering an immediate taxing point. However, the last point has the potential for major tax consequences to the owners when they take money out of the company as a loan. That action triggers very stringent taxation laws. These laws outline how that money is to be paid back within seven, ten or twenty-five years, principal and interest (just like money borrowed from a bank). Failure for the business to comply will result in an unfranked (non-tax) dividend deemed to be paid to the individual. In other words, the individuals are accruing a tax bill that they will have to pay.

The purpose of these laws is to stop business owners from achieving a tax benefit based on the difference between their personal marginal tax rate, potentially close to 50%, and the company tax rate of 30%. To explain further, if the company pays tax at 30% and the business owner uses the profits, after tax, for personal use, she potentially obtains the benefit of a company tax rate (30%).

This issue can become a sleeping giant for businesses and can lead to the demise of the financial position of the owner and the company. Most often this has been seen when people use company funds to pay for deposits on their home or investments when they have not made a plan to pay the loan back. My advice is, get advice. You don't want to get this wrong.

> **SUCCESS TIP**
> Do not use the company bank account for personal uses.

The most regular reason that tends to put people into this situation is that they do not like paying personal tax at higher rates. They know that if they pay themselves salary and wages, they have to pay the appropriate tax within the short term (say, within twelve months). It seems that this is unpalatable for some business owners.

An alternative is to pay a dividend to the owners. The benefit of paying a dividend rather than a salary and wage is that it can defer the tax liability on the dividend until the owner has to pay income tax when she has to lodge the tax return. A dividend can be franked, partially franked or unfranked. If a dividend is franked, it means that there has been tax paid on the dividend by the company. Not wishing to bore you too much or turn you into an accountant, (to do so may mean I have to strip you of your personality. I can say that because I am an accountant) but I am going to spend time explaining to you how franking (the Imputation System) works. Many business owners I have come across do not understand the Imputation System, and I have found that business owners appreciate it when I explain the details, because then they understand how to plan better and legitimately minimise their tax.

This is a typical conversation around imputations:

A company makes a profit of $1m. (Yes, I know that would be nice.)

The company will then have to pay $300,000 in tax since the tax rate is 30%. What is left over is known as the retained profits, $700,000. This profit can be used to continue to grow the business. However, an alternative is that some, or all of it, can be paid as a dividend to shareholders.

What happens when it is paid as a dividend? Let's say that we paid the full retained earnings out as a dividend. (That's just because the math is easier to understand. By the way, most people think that accountants are good at math. Let me tell you that it is not a pre-requisite. I was terrible at math. To be a good accountant you need to know how to add, subtract, divide and multiply. Have you heard the accounting joke—People from different professions are asked, 'What is 1 + 1?' All respond '2'. The accountant's response: 'What would you like it to equal?') Sorry, I got distracted again. The answer is as follows.

Given that the retained earnings have been fully taxed, the dividend paid to the shareholder of the company will be a fully franked dividend. Let's say that there is only one shareholder of the company and he receives 100% of the retained earnings, that is, $700,000. A fully franked dividend is added to the other income of the individual shareholder and he will pay tax on all of the income including the dividend at the personal marginal tax rates.

If the individual already has other income to the value of $180,000, then the dividend will be taxed at the top marginal tax rate of 45% (excluding Medicare). Some people are very concerned that they would have to pay tax of $315,000 ($700,000 × 45%). However, what actually happens due to the imputation system is that they will only pay $150,000 in tax, which represents an effective tax rate of 21.4% on the retained earnings.

So how do we arrive at these numbers?

If I clear the smoke and mirrors some accountants use to explain this, I feel the simplest way to understand it is that if you consider the starting profit of the company ($1m), and you consider that if the individual shareholder would have to pay tax of 45% on the profit, or $450,000, and the company has already paid $300,000 of tax on the $1m profit, then the individual shareholder has to pay the balance, $150,000, (which is $450,000 - $300,000).

You may have worked out that there is no benefit in having a company for tax purposes, because between the company, and you the business owner, you will be paying tax at your applicable marginal income tax rate. This is correct; however, there can be a timing benefit of paying the dividend in a later year than the profit is generated which can assist in cash flow. There can also be a permanent tax saving by deferring the dividend so it is paid in a year when you, the business owner, have lower other income, which may reduce the marginal rate applied to your dividend.

Are you still with me? Did I lose you on this? Hopefully you are still there, because in the words of *Willy Wonka*, 'We have so much time and so little to do. Wait a minute. Strike that. Reverse it!'

What does all that mean from a tax minimisation perspective? It means that a company can better manage its cash flow and working capital cash reserves because it can plan on when the tax, and how much tax, will be paid. (I will unpack this point in Chapter 6.) It means that the business owner can manage when they pay profits to owners without compromising the cash reserves of the business. It also allows there to be a potential timing benefit of deferring tax payments to later years or a permanent difference by timing when the dividends are to be paid in a year when less personal income is received.

Discretionary (Family) Trusts

Trusts go in and out of favour with business owners and their advisors from a tax planning perspective. My view is that trusts have always been and still can be used as effective taxation vehicles if used appropriately and effectively. The reason for varying views of whether they are good or bad is usually due to a lack of knowledge on their purpose and how to effectively use them.

As we've already seen, discretionary trusts have significant asset protection advantages; they also have excellent taxation benefits. A trust can distribute profits to eligible beneficiaries. If there is no eligible beneficiary or if the trustee so chooses, the trustee can retain the profits of the trust and the trustee will be liable for the tax at the top marginal tax rate (that is, 45% plus levies). In most situations, unless there is a strategic decision to retain the profit, the profit will be distributed to eligible beneficiaries to minimise tax and provide a benefit to the beneficiaries.

As a business can be operated in a discretionary trust structure, the profit can be distributed to one or multiple beneficiaries. Remember, the trustee has discretion as to whom to distribute the profit. There is no restriction on who receives the profits as long as they are an eligible beneficiary. The person/s who receives the profits this year do not have to receive the profits in the following year.

The benefit of being able to distribute to multiple beneficiaries is to potentially reduce the quantum of tax payable by spreading the distribution to individuals on lower marginal tax rates. Care must be taken when choosing beneficiaries, as these individuals will be entitled to the distribution amount. There have been situations where profits have been distributed 'on paper' to the children of the business controllers. Whilst this can be effective if the child is not a minor, the issue is that the child is entitled to also have the physical cash distributed. As there is usually insufficient cash in the trust to pay the beneficiaries, there will be a liability on the balance sheet owing to the child. The issue with this is that I have heard of children (or disgruntled former spouses of children) who have successfully sued their parent's trust to obtain the money that was legally owed to them.

A way of avoiding this from happening is ensuring that all expenses paid for on behalf of the children are credited to this loan account. The other way to avoid this is to be nice to your children and teach them good morals and ethics!

Just in case you were wondering if it might be a good idea to have more children as they can be used as a tax minimisation strategy, if you distribute to children under the age of eighteen, the children will be taxed at higher rates. So it only becomes attractive to distribute to them once they become eighteen and before they start to earn significant income generated from their own efforts.

> **SUCCESS TIP**
> Make sure that you distribute profits from the trust to the appropriate eligible beneficiaries with the intention of paying the profits in the future.

There can be restrictions based on the distribution of certain types of income. For example, if the profits of a trust are largely generated from the personal exertion of individuals acting in their own capacity, based on the Personal Services Income (PSI) tax law provisions, the trustee will be required to distribute 100% of the profit generated from these activities to the individual generating it.

The current landscape in Australia is that it is becoming quite difficult to operate trusts tax effectively; there are very strict rules around the distribution of certain types of income and the requirement to declare the distributions at the end of the financial year. If you choose a trust structure to operate your business, then make sure that you have the knowledge or engage advisors who have the knowledge to ensure that you remain compliant and not fall foul of the statutory bodies like the Australian Taxation Office (ATO).

Unit Trusts

The taxation of unit trusts is similar to discretionary trusts in that the beneficiaries will be taxed on the profit distributed. The major difference is that the entitlements of each unit holder are fixed based on their percentage of ownership. The tax rate and the ultimate tax paid on the profit will depend on the type of entity holding the units, for example individual, trust or company.

There can be a benefit in that each unit holder is able to deal with their taxation affairs separately based on their own circumstances. However, this can cause an issue when there is a capital contribution requirement to finance working capital. What I mean is that some unit holders need more cash to pay the tax than others, and the business will continue to be funded to grow, so this may cause pressure on the cash flow of the business.

In case there is any doubt, Australia's tax regime is one of the largest and most complex in the Western world. My earlier disclaimer is critical—please get ongoing specific specialist advice.

Equity and Finance

Cash is king! Cash is the lifeblood of a business; without it the business will not function. So it is imperative that there is sufficient cash available to fund the operations of the business. I will go into more depth about how to effectively and efficiently manage cash in Chapter 6.

Many, many times I have seen businesses fail, not because they didn't have a great idea or a great strategy, but because they didn't forecast the cash requirements of the business appropriately. Most consider this to be an issue when the business commences; however, it is an issue throughout each phase of the business journey.

One of the first questions I ask when determining the appropriate structure of a business is about the owner's succession plan. Effectively, I am starting with the end in mind. I cover this in more detail in the next part of this chapter. But for now, it's critical to consider the need for capital in the business and how the business will be funded, both now and in the future.

There are two types of funding: debt and equity. There are instruments that convert debt to equity, which I will not cover in this book due to the complexity—and to ensure that I don't put you to sleep forever. Debt is where funds are lent to the business and require repayment over a period of time with interest. Equity, or capital, is the injection of funds into the business resulting in ownership of the business.

It is imperative that you consider which option is appropriate for your business now and in the future. If you are self-funding, then a small capital contribution with a loan is usually the main way people fund the business. This is so they can withdraw the cash from the business when there are sufficient funds available without the complexity of returning capital.

If you are seeking funds from other sources, you have the following broad alternatives:

- Personal injection of savings as loan or capital
- Loan from a financial institution
- Loan from a private party
- Capital injection from a related or non-related party

All structures cope with the injection of funds from you, the business owner, into the business, whether you are a sole trader, partnership, trust or company. However, the rules for each structure do differ. There are also multiple ways of raising capital from external parties which will be dependant upon multiple factors including the amount of capital required, for example:

- Venture Capital Fund
- Equity Crowdfunding Platform
- Initial Public Offers

Again, I repeat the earlier disclaimer—please get specialist advice.

You can also obtain finance from a lending institution, such as a bank. Banks will almost always require some form of security when lending money, over either the assets of the business or personal assets of the business owners, such as property. There are so many different types of facilities offered that it would be a book in itself to describe. Suffice it to say, it is worth engaging the appropriate advice when the need arises to finance.

A loan from a private party could come from someone you know, or don't know. If it is from someone you know, generally the terms are fairly reasonable and in line with bank interest. If the loan is from someone that you don't know, it is usually as a last resort because you are unable to get financing from traditional sources. As such, the interest rate is extremely high, which generally reflects the risk of the lender receiving the return of the funds. Once again, all types of structures can receive loans.

Capital injection from related or non-related parties presents a more complex problem depending on the entity in question. This is where you effectively contribute money to own part of the business. The best way to explain this is to consider each entity separately.

Another person cannot own a sole trader business because they can't legally own you. A person who wants to own part of a sole trading business effectively creates a partnership. The contribution into the partnership entitles the person to the agreed proportion of the income and capital of the partnership. The major issue with a partnership is every time the partnership interest changes, it is deemed the dissolution and reconstitution of the partnership. This effectively means that the change in ownership becomes a taxation event. This can become an issue when you want to introduce new partners/investors along the journey and require investment in the business rather than purchasing a portion of the interest from the existing partners.

Funds invested into a company form part of the share capital of the company. Effectively, the investor is purchasing shares. The purchase of shares can come from the company allotting new shares to the investor so the money is injected into the company, or the investor can purchase shares directly from the existing shareholders. If the shares are purchased from the existing shareholders, the funds are paid to the shareholder and not the company. So this is not a funding strategy for the company; it is more a succession planning strategy for the existing owners. A unit trust works the same way as a company in this regard.

The decision as to how to fund the business will be partially decided by the business owners and partially by the people with the funds. If individuals are coming together to own and operate the business initially, then there will be an agreement on the percentage of ownership and the level of funds required to be injected as a loan or as a capital contribution. If there are to be silent investors, the business owner may prefer to retain ownership and seek loans from these people. The downside to this is that there will usually be a greater obligation on the business and potentially personally on the individuals behind the business to pay the loan back, particularly if a personal guarantee is provided.

The choice between loan and equity comes down to risk and reward. Obtaining a loan has a lower risk and higher reward for the business owner because they are not giving up equity in the business. On the other hand, equity has potentially higher risk and lower reward because there is no obligation for the company and the individuals to pay the money back, but the owners have to give up equity.

This situation can arise throughout the life of the business, depending on the funding requirements. Usually an event will trigger the need for funds. So the main point to consider is how much flexibility you require around funding the business in the future. If there is a strong requirement for obtaining future funding from a capital-raising event, this is more effectively managed through company and unit trust structures. If you are looking to obtain Government Grant Funding or access the Research and Development (R&D) Tax Incentive, then you also need to consider the appropriate structure. For example, R&D Tax Incentives can only be accessed by companies.

A discretionary trust does not have the ability to raise capital, as there is no concept of equity entitlement. One of the ways to make this work is to have multiple family trusts coming together as a partnership of trusts. This structure, whilst having some great capital gains tax benefits, can, however, have some significant practical trading issues. Again, specialist advice is recommended.

The whole purpose of an appropriate funding strategy is to ensure that you do not run out of runway. You don't want the business to crash before it even takes off.

> **SUCCESS TIP**
> Make sure that you choose an appropriate structure to ensure that it provides the flexibility to cope with the funding requirements over the life of the business.

Succession Planning

The purpose of a business is to create a new life—a new life that is not dependent upon anyone or anything. A true business is one that exists independent of its owners. There are degrees of reliance upon owners; however, the less reliant upon the owners it is, the higher the value that it will command.

I am often asked how to value a business. Like any asset of value, the value will be determined by what someone is prepared to pay. For some assets, the value is known at any given time because there is a constant market determining price. The best example of this is the stock exchange. But where there is no trading market to determine the value of an SME, we need to use another method to value a business. The most common method in valuing a business is known as the Earning Based Method (EBM).

The EBM is based on the following equation:

$$\text{FME} \times \text{Capitalisation Rate} = \text{Value}$$

FME = Future Maintainable Earnings

Capitalisation Rate = The risk associated with earning the FME in future years

The FME is calculated using the Earnings Before Interest and Tax adjusted for transactions unique to the owners of the business, for example, excess or underpayment of the director's remuneration. So it effectively is the commercial profit of the business operated by an independent person.

The capitalisation rate is the factor assessing the risk of the FME being achieved in the future. If there is a high certainty that the profit will be achieved for a number of years in the future, the capitalisation rate is high. If there is a significant risk that the FME will not be achieved in the following years, the capitalisation rate is low. The more that business can reduce the risk, the higher the capitalisation rate and therefore the higher the value. Most SMEs will command a capitalisation rate of two to five times. There are some businesses that command ten-plus times. Entertainment gaming venues command ten times due to the nature of the demand for the products and services it sells. Internet-based businesses have recorded twenty times and higher, due to the limited barriers of selling products and services which are not restricted by personnel and geographic location.

A business that is reliant on the owners for the profit to be generated in the future may command a one to three times capitalisation rate multiple, whereas businesses that are not reliant upon the owners and are not affected by changing circumstances with customers and employees will command a four to five times capitalisation rate. There are a lot of factors that need to be taken into consideration when determining the capitalisation rate. This book explores the key factors because they help you learn how to increase your business's value.

Some people become uncomfortable when I talk about succession planning, usually because they do not have any plans for selling the business. My response to this is that you don't have to sell just because you create a business that can be sold. The focus here is having a choice. If you build a business with the view of being able to sell it, it focuses your mind on ensuring that you create as much value as possible. Once you have created the value, it provides you with the opportunity to determine if you would like to continue operating the business at a strategic level, that is, working on the business rather than in the business, or sell it, if you are ready to monetise your efforts.

If you are ready to sell, there are a number of options available:

- Trade sale to a competitor or aligned business
- Management buyout by internal staff
- Sale to another business investor
- Listing on the stock exchange

So why is structuring important when it comes to succession planning?

If the value of the business is realised, and there is a profit on the sale of the business, then the Capital Gains Tax (CGT) provisions will apply. If you have the correct structure, there can be significant tax savings under various CGT concessions.

When a profit on a sale occurs, assessment of the assets is required to determine the class of assets. Some are deemed capital, and some are deemed revenue. This is an important distinction because revenue assets will not be eligible for the CGT discounts.

Assuming that you are an individual sole trader, and you have sold the goodwill in your business for $1m, if there were no CGT exemptions available, then the $1m sale, less the cost of the sale, would be added to your income and then taxed. So if you earn greater than $180,000 in other income and the capital gain was $1m, then you would have to pay $450,000 in tax ($1m x 45% top marginal tax rate—excluding Medicare etc.). If you have owned the business for longer than twelve months, then you may be eligible for a 50% discount on the capital gain, known as the CGT general discount. Given the same circumstance above, it would reduce the CGT from $450,000 to $225,000. Given that this is what the tax rules define as a 'small' business, further exemptions apply to the sale which could reduce the CGT to nil. Yes, that is correct, to nil. This may be done using the following Small Business CGT Concessions:

- The 15-year rule

- 50% Active Asset Exemption

- Retirement Exemption

- Active Asset Rollover

I have regularly applied these Small Business CGT Concessions for customers with great success.

Because we are working within tax laws, the application of the provisions to your circumstance is quite difficult. If I explained them fully, you would definitely have a very deep sleep. Suffice it to say, (again), you need to speak to a specialist to ensure that your specific circumstances are taken into consideration when assessing your eligibility to minimise your tax payments.

An individual is able to access the CGT general discount and the Small Business CGT Concessions, as is a business trading as a discretionary trust. However, there are further layers of eligibility criteria applicable to the trust.

A company entity does not enjoy the same level of CGT benefits as individuals or discretionary trusts. Yet the shareholders may be able to obtain the same benefits if certain criteria are met. The company is not eligible for the 50% general discount, but it is eligible for some of the Small Business CGT Concessions. If the shareholder is an individual or a trust and shares are sold rather than the assets from the company, then the exemptions will apply if all the eligibility criteria are met.

If a unit trust structure is used and the assets are sold from the unit trust, then it will be eligible for the general discount and the small business CGT concessions. The unit trust will have a better result than the company, but not as good as if the business was sold by the individual or the discretionary trust. If the units are sold by an individual or discretionary trust, then the same result applies as a shareholder in a company.

The CGT applicable to a partnership will depend on who the partners are, as the tax consequences rest with the partners and not the partnership. A partnership of discretionary trusts or individuals will more likely be eligible for all of the exemptions, as compared to a partnership of companies.

By way of providing something to take away from this chapter and to give you some direction, the structure that we most often use is a company to trade the business and a discretionary family trust to own the shares of the company. This structure has excellent asset protection features, ensures limited liability, enjoys the corporate rate of tax, has the most flexibility when it comes to financing and raising capital and, under certain circumstances, can be eligible for the CGT exemptions—if the shares rather than the assets are sold. However, this structure is not for everyone and can be costly to set up. So it is best to check with your advisor before making the decision as to what is best for your personal circumstances.

Now you have a working knowledge about structuring to seek the answers you need from your own advisor. The other benefit is that now you will be able to wow your mates at the next barbecue with your knowledge.

Shareholders Agreements

For completeness, and while it is outside the scope of this book, it is important to note that once a structure has been determined, if it is with multiple owners, there should be an agreement drawn up to outline the rules on how the entity and the business should be run. It is similar to a prenuptial for a couple before they get married. It is better to set out the rules when everyone is talking, as compared to when everyone is in dispute. There is also the ability to connect insurance through the addition of cover equal to the value of an owner's interest in the business.

Chapter 4

HOW DO WE CHART THE COURSE?

The Financial Map

So far in this book, you have read through some of the basics for an overall view of business and how you might structure it appropriately. Now it's time to talk numbers.

There are two types of people in the world: those who like and are interested in financial information and those who are not. What I have found is that the people who do not like reading business numbers are people who have not been given the opportunity to learn how to properly do so. In practice, even my most defiant customers who initially did not want to know anything about the financial health of their company—or lack thereof—once educated, now enjoy reading this information, and are in fact excited about it. The trick is to start off small and get them used to a couple of business indicators so they understand the importance. Then gradually show them how to read, interpret and analyse the information they are presented.

One of my favourite experiences in business is seeing business owners go from not wishing to open the financial reports that I present, to eagerly opening and reading the reports before I've even had the chance to present. Everyone is capable of reading, interpreting and analysing financial information; they just have to be properly shown how.

> **SUCCESS TIP**
> If you don't like reading financial information, seek people who can teach you to understand. You may find that you actually like numbers once you are shown how.

In this chapter I am going to step through how to start charting the course of your business from a financial perspective. This is where we start to link the strategy to the outcome. Remember the analogy that I have been using in this book about travel? Well, what I am about to do is explain how you set the map. Remember that the map is the strategy to get you towards your vision, Why or destination. Often I find there is a significant gap that exists between the goals set out in a business plan and the way business owners operate their businesses. The missing link is an implementation plan. Most of my time is spent teaching business owners how to set the plan and then concentrate on how to implement the plan. Regularly, business owners will write magnificent business plans that sit on the shelf. People start operating the business without consulting these plans again. Often the plans are too conceptual, so they are difficult to implement. This is the main reason I spend considerable time writing implementation plans. The trick is to use tools that do not require a laborious amount of time to prepare and use. As business owners, you are time-poor. You don't have the luxury of spending time 'planning'. You need to spend every bit of your time early on in your business life 'doing'. As the business grows and develops, your time will be freed up to work more on your business, but early on it is tough.

Budgeting

Part of the business planning process is to complete a budget. All business owners at one point in their lives have struggled with completing a budget. Why is this the case? The answer is simple. We can't predict the future. So unless we have been blessed with abilities to see into the future, we may find it hard to know the best steps to take in business.

Let's break this down further. What part of the budget do we find easier to complete than other parts? Most people can predict the future costs of the business because they are more finite and known. The struggle is predicting the future sales. Business owners of established businesses may find it easier to predict the future sales as compared to start-ups because businesses that have been around for a while can look back on past and current sales. However, as noted in Chapter 1, history is not always a good measure of the future, especially in our rapidly changing global economy. Moreover, the future of some businesses is easier to predict than others. When businesses have long-term contracts with customers or strong relationships with their customers, they usually enjoy more predictability than businesses that don't.

For simplicity, business models can fall into two groups: relationship and transaction-based businesses. A relationship business is one where customers will continually and regularly purchase your services and products. A transactional business relies on one-off purchases from your business. In some businesses there is a blend of both. For example, real estate agents have a very transactional business, where most of their customers will buy from them once. (This highlights the difference between relationship-based businesses and transactional-based businesses. Particularly, how transactional businesses need to budget knowing that the revenue is unpredictable. If the statistic 'on average, people will purchase real estate every seven years' is partly true, then this focuses how the real estate agent needs to manage success, in particular, that there needs to be a strong focus on good relationships outside the immediate customer.) So you can see that it would be hard to predict the future sales in real estate. However, there are customers of real estate agents that would buy more regularly when a stronger relationship is cultivated, such as property developers. Also, people are more likely to recommend a real estate agent whom they trust and have built a rapport with.

A great example of a relationship business is an accounting firm. There is a greater likelihood that customers of an accounting firm will continue to buy the services based on the relationship. Another type of business may be a subscription-based model, where people sign up to contracts over a period of time. Contracts provide a high degree of certainty of future revenue. What is not certain is the level of renewals of the contracts.

Because business owners find it hard to predict the future, they tend to budget conservatively. They will increase the income and expenses by 10%. So if they did $1m in sales last year, then they forecast they will do $1.1m this year. The issue that arises here is that there is absolutely no accountability to reach that goal. When I sit down with customers for a 'business owners' monthly review', to see if they are on track with their budget, I will ask why there is a variance. More often than not, they are not sure. Just to highlight the point, it is not just about getting the forecast correct, it's about the reasons why there is a variance. If the only reason is because they just set the sales figures to increase by a percentage, then there is not a lot of information to tell from the variance. This is because the forecast is arbitrary. Perhaps you've already worked it out, but I am reasonably set on my thoughts with my customers about this point.

Using travel analogy, setting a budget based on an arbitrary measure such as a percentage increase, is like having two points on the map: the starting point and a town somewhere further along the way. You would struggle to navigate there, as the path is not clear. However, if you are clear on the components that make up the total sales, these become your roads and road signs—that is, your signals. This sounds so simple, yet most business owners do not do this well (if at all). They know that they have to do it, even ought to do it, but they just don't. But when they do, the results are awesome. This is why I focus on analysing streams of income, because it makes such a difference to the business—and goes a long way towards helping you achieve your ultimate business goal.

> **SUCCESS TIP**
> Don't just focus on the total sales when forecasting; focus on how to achieve the sales forecast.

The only time that I accept setting a budget using a percentage increase is as a starting point. Budgeting is about setting an outcome. What result do you want to achieve? The most important number on a budgeted profit and loss statement is the profit. You need to assess whether this is acceptable. To establish the appropriate budgeted profit, I use a top-down, bottom-up approach. Top-down is where you start with projected sales, which may be a percentage increase from last year, and determine the applicable expenses to establish a forecasted profit. Once we have completed the top-down, I then look at the profit to see if it is what the business owner wants to ultimately achieve that year. If not, then I work backwards, or bottom-up, to determine what the sales and expenses have to be to get the results. Once this process is complete, then we plan how we achieve it. This is where the sales component becomes a relevant focus.

Once we complete the budgeted profit and loss, we turn this into a forecasted cash flow statement. Whilst determination of the profit is very important, the most important number that you need to track in a business is cash. Is there enough cash to operate the business and provide a return on the owner's investment in the business? We will discuss cash in Chapter 6.

Clearly every business, industry and stage of business life presents challenges for forecasting sales. Because we face this problem every day, I have developed a model that assists business owners in taking some of the guesswork out of forecasting.

The main motivation for developing this model is because business owners have a great resistance to putting numbers on a page. If they do so, they know they'll be held accountable to those numbers or—worse still—if they don't achieve those numbers, they'll have to face failure. Here is the thing about forecasting and budgeting: it is extremely rare that you will exactly achieve your budget. You may exceed it or not achieve it at all. But you need to have a goal. The real benefit comes from the information that rises to the surface by examining the variances that exist against the budget. If you are under- or overachieving your forecast, there will be reasons. The reasons provide you with the knowledge to establish a clearer direction for the future.

SUCCESS TIP
No matter how difficult preparing a budget is, there is no excuse for a lack of preparation. Without it, you are flying blind.

As forecasting sales is the trickiest part of preparing a budget, we are going to spend some time going over how we can better prepare forecasts. There are a number of factors we need to consider.

As you have gathered by now, I like to simplify what is perceived to be complex. I am always seeking ways to explain the complex in simple terms and looking for tools to assist business owners in implementing plans in a fast and effective manner.

A large part of strategy is about figuring out how to grow your business. Therefore we need to adopt strategies that increase sales in your business.

The model that I teach my customers is formulating a budget around their sales and marketing implementation plan. Most businesses complete a forecast on spreadsheets. This is also my preferred tool; it allows great flexibility when completing financial modelling. There are numerous financial software packages that assist with the process of financial modelling; however, most have limitations that I find frustrating. Also, because business owners are time-poor, I like to use tools that are quick to learn and will focus on the implementation of it. That's why I keep coming back to Microsoft Excel.

The most efficient and effective way of preparing budgets in Excel is to download your profit and loss statement from your accounting package into Excel. Almost every accounting software package has this ability (usually something along the lines of 'export file as a .CSV file'; this is what you are looking for). This export becomes your summary budgeted profit and loss statement. You can then create additional Excel pages behind this initial summary page that supports the detail and assumptions of the forecast summary page. The first worksheet page that you should create, after the forecast page, is the 'Sales and Marketing' page. This becomes your sales and marketing implementation plan page. If you are in business or just about to commence, you need a sales and marketing strategy. Unfortunately, often in practice, this plan is in the head of the business owner and not on paper. It makes it very difficult to chart the course when no one else can see those thoughts. That's why I've developed this model.

I am discussing this as if you have commenced business, but the same principles apply to start-ups. Existing businesses can also use it as a litmus test.

One of the philosophies that I adopt when budgeting is based on the fundamentals of how to grow a business. I came across a very simple way to consider how to grow your business that was explained by U.S. sales and marketing expert Jay Abraham.

Abraham explains that there only three ways to grow a business:

1. Increase the **number of customers**
2. Increase the **average transaction value**
3. Increase the **number of transactions per year**

Here is a worked example on what this all means:

Imagine your business has 300 customers and on average they buy from you six times per year. If the average price of each transaction is $500, then the total income for the year is $900,000. To better understand this concept, we need to break down the total number of sales to the factors that make up this number. Focusing effectively on the sales and marketing aspects show us how to increase the total revenue of the business. This step breaks down the sales and marketing plan into projects and actions that must be undertaken to achieve the budgeted sales in the coming months.

Note: Sales is direct income from the sale of the product or service that the business sells, while revenue is the total income from all sources that the business generates (for example, interest from cash at the bank, or income from patents or book sales as well as sales income.)

Let's look at each component to determine how to build the model and link your sales and marketing plan with your budget to ensure that you have a sales and marketing implementation action plan.

1. Increase the Number of Customers

First, you need to understand the number of customers that you have and how to attract more. This involves analysing the following:

(i)   The number of customers you have now

(ii)   The number of customers you lose

(iii) The number of leads from prospective customers you attract

(iv)   The rate you convert leads into customers

Each of these points will be discussed in more depth below.

i. The Number of Customers You Have Now

People reading this book, who are just about to commence business, may find this concept difficult, however, it is important to understand for the longer term benefit of your business. Business owners who have been trading for a period of time do not always know how many current customers they have. From a rational perspective this seems ridiculous, but from a business owner's perspective this is normal. Why? Because, as the business gets bigger, it becomes harder to know every aspect of your business. With this statement, I potentially give every business owner an excuse not to understand these numbers. Nevertheless, while there are some things I am less rigid on, when it comes to business owners not knowing the details, I have found there are certain details that if the business owner does not know or understand, they are much more likely to fail in their business. One of the details that are a non-negotiable for business owners knowing is their critical numbers. Critical numbers are the indicators that will measure business success.

The issue that arises when business owners don't know the number of customers they have is that it means that the starting point in a journey is unknown. Again, using the travel analogy, if you want to travel to Sydney by car and you think you are in Melbourne, you will set your map around these two points. But if think you are in Melbourne, and you really are in Adelaide, the map will be useless. Make sure that you know what your starting point is before commencing the journey.

One of these critical numbers is how many customers currently buy from you. Some of you will ask what constitutes a current customer. My response to this is a customer is someone who has bought from you in the last twelve months and has not indicated that they no longer want to buy from you. In some businesses that number will not be 100% accurate unless you survey your customers every day on when they are going to buy from you.

So what makes up the number of customers? What should we measure to determine the number of customers? There will be existing customers who continually buy from you, new customers who are starting to buy from you and customers who have indicated they no longer want to buy from you.

ii. The Number of Customers You Lose

Before we talk about attracting new customers, it is more appropriate to determine your existing customers. Knowing how many existing customers you have means that you need to know if you are losing customers. Are the names on your customer list still customers? If you are currently losing 20% of your customers per year and you can implement policies to stop half of them from leaving by providing better service and improving relationship management and communications, it is the equivalent of gaining an extra 10% of new customers each year (the maths is as follows: 20% loss x 50% improvement = 10% lost and now 90% retained).

Growing by improving your retention rates does not require expensive and risky advertising and can be relatively easily done when you start focusing on why customers are leaving. To determine the retention rate of your customers, print off a list of your customers from the prior financial year and a list of your customers from your current financial year. Compare and assess how many customers who bought from you in the previous year did not buy from you in the current year. You divide this number of lost customers into the total number of customers that bought from you in the previous financial year to determine the retention rate percentage.

What does a retention rate percentage actually measure, and why is it important to determine? It should be noted that this ratio is not relevant for transactional non-relationship style businesses that will only buy from you once. If the business you operate is a relationship-based business where customers buy from you continuously (or at minimum annually), then this ratio is extremely important. It is important because it can be a measure of customer satisfaction. If customers are leaving you and going to competitors, this is a reflection of their experience with you. However, sometimes it can be a reflection that they no longer need your products and services. Knowing why they are leaving is the key. It could be due to price, expectation or need. To elaborate on these points, you may be too expensive, you might not have met or exceeded their expectations relating to the product or service, they might not have enjoyed the experience your business provides or they may no longer need your product or service.

The percentage alone is just a measure; the power of the statistic comes from knowing why the ratio is what it is. Sometimes there are industry statistics that you can benchmark yourself against to see if you are above or below the industry average. This can normalise the statistic; however, don't forget the average is the middle point of a range. Being in the middle is boring and mediocre; what you want to benchmark your business against is the top 20% of performers in your industry.

Even if you don't have industry statistics, the power comes from knowing what is going on in your business that you can improve upon. If customers are leaving you because you are not servicing them well, then you have the power to effect change. It becomes the catalyst for change. To find out why your customers are leaving you, call them and find out. This will provide you with the knowledge to make changes in your business and reduce the number of customers who leave. Then your retention ratio will increase, and you'll end up with more customers.

Why is this so important for forecasting purposes? This will assist you in determining how many customers are likely to buy from you in the future. Because if you have a certain number of customers at the end of the year, by applying the ratio, you can determine approximately how many of those customers will buy from you in the future. It also provides you with a benchmark that allows you to track improvement.

To round off this conversation, sometimes a decreasing retention rate is not a bad thing. You may want to lose customers who are not the right fit for your business. My tip to you is rather than telling these customers to go somewhere else, or service them poorly so they leave of their own free will, identify them, and see if you can place them with another business that is more likely to suit their needs. Potentially you could gain financially by selling this client base to another more appropriate provider.

iii. The Number of Leads from Prospective Customers You Attract

Now that you know how many existing customers you have, you need to consider how to grow your customer portfolio. The reality is, if your retention rate is anything less than 100%, your business is in decline, unless you are acquiring new customers. There are two distinct ways to acquire new customers. You can purchase a business (instantly increasing your customers) or you can increase through sales and marketing.

There are two types of customers: ones that currently buy from you and the ones that don't. This is a bit tongue-in-cheek, because the ones that don't are not your customers yet. They are prospects—customers who haven't bought from you yet.

If you are starting your business, you don't have customers, you have prospects. In fact, you have a whole world of prospects! If you have been trading your business, you will have prospects and customers.

Let's take a closer look at marketing. If you are anything like me, marketing has always seemed to be a difficult term to define and understand in a practical sense. I even used to put sales and marketing together as one and the same, which is a bit embarrassing considering I minored in marketing at university (must be the accountant in me). On reflection, it would seem that the reason I put the terms together was because sales and marketing are both required to grow your business. Then I discovered I could use outcomes to explain the terms in a simple way.

Marketing is about driving a prospect to your door. The whole purpose of marketing is to generate leads to your business. Marketing is all about determining who, out of your target audience (or prospects), is a likely customer. Once you have determined that, you need your target audience to become aware of your business so that you become known. Once you have become known to your audience, this will generate interest, so when your audience has a need for the products you sell, they are more likely to choose to buy from you. If you have competitors, the prospect is choosing to buy from you rather than from your competitors.

The main purpose of the sales process is to convert the audience that has shown interest in your products or services to buy from you. A great sales process will turn a prospect into a customer, which we cover next in conversion.

The best measure for marketing is the number of leads that are generated. The measure in your business may be how many buying enquiries you have had in a particular period. A period may be a week, month, quarter or year. Marketing is about becoming known to your target audience. The corner piece to this is branding. Branding is the image of your business that you are communicating to the world. The best test to know if branding works is if the right prospects are knocking on your door. If not, you need to review, check and adjust your communications with the world. You may have your brand right, but you may not be communicating it correctly or to your target audience.

My experience with marketing is that it is all about testing and measuring. There are no silver bullets in marketing, especially in the changing world that we live in. The other key to marketing is ensuring that there is constant and consistent communication. One email or one offer is not sufficient to deliver an outstanding result. Especially when we live in a world of an abundance of choices, competitors and information (a great read on this is *The Paradox of Choice: Why More Is Less* by Barry Schwartz). Also consider that a confused prospect is a lost prospect. Keep your message simple and clear.

Once again you need to know how many leads you are currently generating in your business. If you don't know, then you need to find out. This can be as simple as every time you get an enquiry, either via the phone, email or social media, you mark it down and then collate the statistics. Some of you will be using a Customer Relationship Management (CRM) program to manage your marketing and sales process. If you are, this is excellent. If you are not, I encourage you to get one if it's applicable. I would argue that if you have customers in your business, you need one. So get a CRM program.

Having said that, many businesses that have a CRM program don't use it effectively. Here is another tip: start using it effectively for the purpose that it was designed for. Its purpose is to provide information to ensure that you drive sales in your business. It provides intelligence on your sales and marketing activity and provides information on the process of converting a prospect into a sale.

The now not-so-latest sensation is digital or social media, to which you need to consider a strategy and implement it in this space. My advice is to be mindful that it is another communication medium to promote your brand and business to drive traffic to your door. Social media is an extremely important marketing tool now and in the future. If you don't have an online presence, you can quickly get left behind. But ask yourself one question: are my prospects online and looking for my products and services? There is a fair chance the answer will be yes, but you need to ask this question first. Then ask, where do they go—and how do they search—to find products and services similar to yours? Answering that question will help you target your communications so they see and hear your message. I am by no means a digital advertising expert, but I certainly use the medium, and I am continually testing and measuring to see where my efforts should be targeted to get the best results.

Determining how many leads you are generating is the starting point to determining how many new customers you will attain.

Growing your business by increasing the number of customers means you'll need to attract more leads from prospects.

That means either or both of the following actions need to be implemented in your business, as noted by Abraham:

a **More effective advertising.** Abraham advocates optimisation and the need to continually test for better, more effective ways to market your business. Improving marketing can create great leverage. If your advertising creates ten leads per week, a better headline and more persuasive offers may generate twenty leads without incurring more costs.

b **More advertising and promotion.** Here, Abraham recommends using *The Power Parthenon* strategy to create multiple sources for leads so you are not reliant on just one. To read more on this and more of Abraham's ideas, his books *Getting Everything You Can Out of All You've Got* and *The Sticking Point Solutions* are a good start, particularly when he currently offers the first book for free on his website.

Here is an example of marketing in its simplest form. The other day I was in the car park of the local shopping centre with my three children, waiting for my wife, Amanda. She had gone to pick up a few things for lunch. Whilst chatting with the kids, I noticed a man in his late twenties in neat gardening attire handing out pamphlets. Instantly, I wondered what he was handing out. As I continued to watch, I observed that he would politely approach people as they passed by, introduce himself, and hand out a pamphlet. Some people took it and others didn't. However, there were many that engaged in conversation with this man.

As I observed his attire and how he engaged with people, I thought, 'He must be promoting his business, which must be something to do with gardening.' I guessed gardening based on the shorts and shoes that he was wearing. Then I noticed Amanda walk towards this fellow and chat with him for a few minutes. When Amanda got back in the car, I asked what the fellow was promoting. She confirmed my guess that he was promoting his garden maintenance business. Then, I asked what he said before he handed her the pamphlet. The answer? 'Hi, I am new to the area, and I am here today promoting my garden maintenance business. Would you be interested in taking one of my pamphlets?' Wow! What an amazingly simple but effective opening line.

So, knowing Amanda, I then asked, 'What time is he coming over?' By the way he had engaged with her, it appeared that he had successfully made a time to provide us with a quote. Sure enough, this fellow—let's call him Gary the gardener—came over to our house that afternoon.

When I met Gary, I was impressed with how genuine and enthusiastic he was regarding what he did and how he could assist us. What he did best was build trust. Based on my experience, the new way of selling is all about trust. Nowadays it's not about closing deals. The deals will close themselves if you build trust. When you are engaging with a potential customer, you should not be thinking about selling, you should be thinking about building trust. Gary did this well with every step along his engagement. The way he looked, the way he engaged and spoke, the fact that he turned up when he said he would. The first thing he said to me was that he was probably blocking the drive and apologised. By the end of the conversation, he had been given a list of things to do, he provided a price and he let us know when he was going to complete the job.

To better understand Gary's business, I asked him about his technique of obtaining new customers. He said that in the past, he had dropped 500 pamphlets into letterboxes. This would result in about five enquiries. In other words, only 1% of the total pamphlets delivered provided Gary with a lead. Conversely, when he set himself up at the local supermarket and handed out fifty pamphlets, he would get at least ten enquiries—that is, 20% of pamphlets handed out created a lead—and usually he could convert 50% of those leads into new customers. So while it took more time, the results were superior. I was extremely impressed with how committed Gary was to getting his business going. People like Gary deserve to do well in business and they usually do. I genuinely felt really pleased for him and was also very happy that he now looked after our property.

> **SUCCESS TIP**
> Marketing is not about selling and closing deals. It is about building trust every time you have the opportunity to engage with potential customers.

iv. The Rate You Convert Leads into Customers

Now that you have prospects showing up at your door, you need to encourage them to buy from you to turn them into customers. This is the point in the sales model where you convert prospects into customers. This is the sales discipline of sales and marketing.

Once again, do you know your current sales conversion rate? If not, you need to start tracking it. My earlier suggestions were that it could be as simple as keeping an Excel spreadsheet or a CRM program. The point is that you need to have a system to track this statistic.

If your conversion rate is less than 100%, there is room for improvement. However, if it is very high, it may not be a focus for you right now. Business is constantly weighing your choices and prioritising where your efforts should be to get the most improvement.

Based on my experience, the reason why sales conversion is poor is due either to the capability of the salespeople or the capability of the business to provide sufficient resources, education, processes or support to the salespeople. The cornerstone of this goes back to the Why that was discussed in Chapter 1. A business should prioritise providing the salespeople with all of the information they need to sell the products and services. Differentiation from competitors is one of the keys.

One day, I was reviewing the financial performance of a customer. There was a considerable negative variance to the budgeted sales figures both for the month, and for the year to date. This suggested there had been a consistent pattern of poor sales performance. Based on this information, my questions to the director of the business were as follows:

Is the low sales performance due to the salespeople being:

- Lazy,
- Incompetent, or
- Not equipped with the knowledge, resources and support by you, the director of the business?

The director did not really know because he was only guessing what the issue was. The reason he did not know was that he had not been tracking the appropriate sales statistics. He was having sales meetings but was not holding the team accountable to the correct Key Performance Indicators (KPIs) to appropriately assess performance. Because he did not know, the appropriate business decision was to keep the salespeople, but monitor them with appropriate KPIs to see if that turned around their performance. Based on using this method, within two months, two salespeople left the business, and the remaining group performed better and beat their budget. Having the statistical (or empirical evidence) to support these types of decisions can allow the business owner to review and analyse what works well and what does not. It can assist with removing some of the emotion from the decision. At the end of the day, if the business is not profitable, no one will have a job. Not knowing the KPIs and not keeping his salespeople accountable resulted in significant liquidity problems, and the company came close to being shut down. Now I am pleased to say the business traded out of its terrible predicament. The director had many sleepless nights, often kicking himself that he should have taken those steps much sooner. However, now that he understands the metrics, he can use those lessons to prevent a similar occurrence in the future.

Don't make the same mistake. My advice is to never employ a salesperson until you have developed a strong infrastructure to support that employee. Make sure that you have a documented sales process and all the tools that you need to assist your salespeople to uniformly and consistently perform.

Another significant reason why salespeople may not be performing and converting sales is due to the quality of the prospects. If the prospects are not ideal, then this can be the cause of a low conversion rate.

Another common issue that SMEs with salespeople face is that the performance of salespeople in a large business is no guarantee of their performance in an SME. Many times my customers have been able to secure the employment of top quality salespeople from large corporations. There is an assumption that because they have performed well in a large business, they will be able to perform well in an SME. Unfortunately, more often than not, the performance does not translate. This is usually for two reasons. One, the salespeople were great performers because the previous business provided them with high-quality resources and support, and they knew how to perform well under those circumstances. If you take that support away, so go the sales. And the second reason is that the previous business had a very strong brand in the marketplace, which consequently affected the salesperson's performance. (Peter Drucker has suggested that if your marketing is spot on, then a sales team can become superfluous. The Soul of Enterprise Podcast has discussed this matter a number of times with interesting insights. In particular, that Drucker did not document this in his books, but did regularly discuss it in his teachings.) An SME will usually employ these top-performing salespersons to help them build the sales infrastructure from the ground up. In this environment it can be an unfortunate result for the SME when it is evident that the salesperson was successful due to their previous business's support, processes and established brand, rather than their independent ability to bring in business.

There are two areas to improve conversion rates: immediate and follow-up.

If you improve the sales skills of your staff, so that they focus on what the customer needs and wants, you should increase the number of customers you create early in the sales process.

It has been suggested that most salespeople give up too early. Sales staff should try to close if the customer appears ready to buy, but if the customer isn't ready, you need a way to educate the customer and build the relationship until they are ready. Google conducted a project around the Zero Moment of Truth; one of the key metrics that they wanted to understand was, 'What does a prospect do to assist them to make the decision to buy?' From that research the findings suggested that, as a general rule, prospects require eleven sources of information. Daniel Priestley takes this further in his book *Oversubscribed,* to suggest that to have people engage with your brand, you also need them to experience up to seven hours of content across four different platforms (for example video, podcast, book and an email).

Bearing this in mind, and that some research indicates that the majority of salespeople give up after the first or second 'No', how often will that salesperson be successful if the product or service that your business is trying to sell does not provide the basic expectation, and if the salesperson stops contacting prospects. It has been suggested that it can take ten or twelve contacts before a prospect converts to a customer. Does this make you rethink how you set up your sales team and what your business needs to provide to allow a higher chance of success for the sales team?

Selling, especially in service-based businesses, is all about building trust. Trust is not built in one phone call or email. It is built by consistently providing value without expecting a sale immediately. Some of my customers think that every time that they have a meeting with a prospect, they have to make a sale. My advice to business owners is to go into every conversation with the object of building trust, not selling. The sale will come if the trust has been built.

This is the basis behind the accelerating sales model. Build trust through initially providing free or low-cost products to provide a taste to your prospects of the benefit of engaging with your business. Once you have built the trust, then you are able to sell your premium products.

> **SUCCESS TIP**
> Don't expect a sale each time you engage with a customer. Build trust and the sale will come.

2. Increase the Average Transaction Value

There are two possible ways to increase the transaction value of each purchase: increase prices or sell more products.

Practical tips of each method are reviewed below.

i. Increasing Your Prices

It is easy to think that price dominates your customers' decisions. This perception is founded on the prospects and customers pushing back on price. However, it may merely be due to the way we all operate in that we always want to think that we are getting a bargain. Negotiating on prices is the modern day commercial battle that exists. Whilst an increase in price can result in a loss of customers, repeated tests show that revenue will increase, because the impact on the increase in price will outweigh the impact of the loss of a customer. Ron Baker suggests that you should not let bad customers drive out good customers, and often pricing will assist in determining who are truly your good customers.

> **SUCCESS TIP**
> Do not automatically dismiss the option to increase price to increase the average transaction value of each sale.

ii. Upselling and Cross-Selling

There is an awesome model that clearly explains the easiest to hardest ways to grow your business. I call it the Business Growth Quadrant. It diagrammatically determines the easiest to hardest ways to grow your business. It is such a simple, but really effective tool in determining the different ways to grow your business.

Picture a box divided into four. In the top two sections of the box, you have your Existing Customers, and on the bottom, you have the New Customers. The left-hand side of the box represents your existing products and services, and the right side represents your new products and services. Looking at the box, you can establish what products/ services (existing or new) you are selling to what customers (existing or new). Now, write a number in each box assessing the easiest to hardest way to grow your business. (One being the easiest, and four being the hardest.) Is it easier or harder to grow the top-left box (existing products to existing customers)? What about new products to existing customers? How about new products to new customers, and new customers to existing products? Rate each box in terms of difficulty, one to four.

There is only one right answer—although I have had people in my workshops argue with me. (This is fine, because I am happy to discuss it until people get it.) If you had one in the top-left box, followed by two in the top-right box, followed by three in the bottom-left box and four in the bottom-right box, then you are correct. Give yourself a gold star.

Business Growth Quadrant

Existing Customers

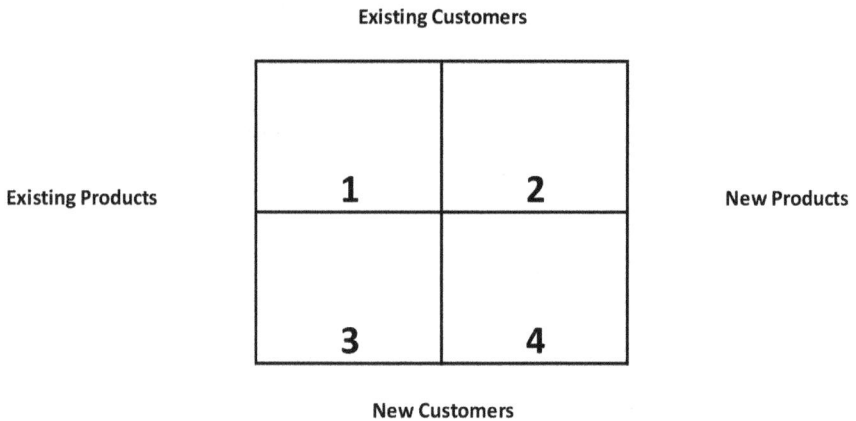

Existing Products | 1 | 2 | New Products

3   4

New Customers

(Image based on Matrix invented by Boston Consulting Group (BCG) in the 1970s)

Let me explain why this is correct. First, it costs many times (suggestions are as small a number as seven to as large as thirty) more to sell to a new customer than it does to sell to an existing customer. Whatever the real statistic is does not really matter. The underlying point is that it is much cheaper and easier to sell to a customer you currently have a relationship with. With respect to quadrant one, you may think that if they are an existing customer buying existing products then selling here could not be considered growth. The question that I ask is, 'Do all your existing customers buy all your existing products?' Sometimes the answer is 'Yes', so it may not be a growth strategy, but more often than not businesses answer 'No' to this question. This presents a wonderful low-cost, easy strategy for growing the business.

While I was recently conducting a monthly directors meeting with one of my customers I said, 'You really need to grow your business, because it is in a critical phase where if you don't, you won't be in business in the next six months.' After the colour came back to the customer's face he said, 'But I hate selling. I feel like a used car salesman.' (Apologies to any used car salesmen who are reading this book. And as a further side point, industries that have a bad name for not being as ethical as others (or 'dodgy') provide a real opportunity for ethical people to stand out and become hugely successful. So if you are in an industry renowned for being a bit dodgy, and you are ethical, you will blow your competitors out of the water.) This customer's issue was a lack of confidence and self-respect in what he did. He was wired to think that 'selling' was a dirty word. So I asked him the following questions:

1. Do you believe in your business?
2. Do you believe that your products and services are better than your competitors'?
3. Do you know that your customers are better off because they buy your products and services?

Thank goodness the customer said 'Yes' to each one of these questions—otherwise there would have been a whole other discussion. My next statement was, 'If you know that people who buy from you have a great experience as compared to your competitors, don't you want to communicate that to the world so all can experience the same?' Once again the answer was 'Yes'. The lesson here is that if you have a fear of selling because you feel it compromises your ethics, then first make sure that you believe in what you sell, and second, rewire your thinking to recognise that you are offering someone the opportunity to have a great experience with you.

In this instance, I could not break the wiring of the business owner in one meeting, so I started him on small steps. I focused on quadrant one and asked if all of his current customers were buying all his products. He admitted that they were not. I gave him this challenge. Before our next meeting, arrange a meeting with all your current customers for the following purposes:

1. Get feedback on their relationship with you—this step is great for retention strategy knowledge

2. Build the customer experience relationship—this is wonderful for customer retention because you're demonstrating that you care

3. Present all of the products in your product range—an easy sales strategy for growing your business

So in one meeting, a great deal of progress can happen. I asked how the business owner felt about having this conversation with his customers. He was super-confident because he did not feel like he was compromising his ethics. What he'd reframed in his mind was that he was helping his customers understand all of his products. The results were phenomenal. Not only did the owner see an increase in sales, get helpful data and build existing relationships, he also gained a better script and mindset when he decided to sell to new prospects.

And that is just from working at quadrant one. See where this is going?

Quadrant two is all about selling new products to existing customers, which is called the distribution model. Customers are one of the most valuable assets in a business. There is a saying, 'He who has the numbers wins the race.' Think about the biggest Internet-based companies in the world: Google, LinkedIn, YouTube, Facebook, etc. These companies have a massive database of users. This gives them tremendous distribution power. Effectively, they can sell pretty much anything in large volumes, because they have existing customers who use their products. The same principle applies to SMEs but on a much smaller basis. The key to selling new products to existing customers is all about understanding what else your customer needs and then see your business as a supplier of this product. In the example provided above, I requested my customer to speak to each one of his customers for multiple reasons. One of these was to test what other products the customers would buy.

In business we often assume things because we don't have all the information. Sometimes this is because there is no source for the information; however, other times there is a source, but we don't have the confidence to go to the source. A vital information-rich source on running a successful business is your customers. When in doubt, don't assume. Ask your customer. Whilst I have proven this to be great advice time and time again, not everyone accepts nor takes action with it. (As a side note, I am not bullish enough to think that all my advice should be taken; however, the successful business owners are usually the ones with open minds, take on board, and think about what was said.) Based on my experience, people sometimes don't want to ask because their customers may give them negative feedback. Whilst this can be hard to accept, it is once again like taking medicine, as it will cure your business problems. You can always turn the negative into a positive and potentially save losing a customer. Another upside is that those customer insights can provide your business with amazing intelligence about creating better products and services for all your customers and attracting new customers.

SUCCESS TIP
If you have a question about your business that you don't really know the answer to, don't assume, and don't be afraid to ask your customer. Even if you think that you know the answer, or even if you don't want to know the answer because it may be negative, still ask.

3. Increasing the Number of Transactions per Year

The last of the three ways to grow a business is to increase the number of transactions per year, or in other words, the number of times a customer buys from you. This requires you to continually meet and exceed the expectations of your customer. It requires you to constantly and consistently deliver on your marketing promises and then keep in contact with your customer. Your competitors are probably talking to them too, so if you stand back and think you have their business, you could be sadly mistaken.

Whilst we are referencing your marketing promises, what is your brand promise? What do you stand for as a business? Identifying this, communicating this and keeping to your promise will help you build trust with your customers. Sometimes a brand promise can come down to a single word. Many companies have been successful in 'owning' certain words. When I say the word 'Toyota', what is the first word that comes to mind? It's usually 'reliable'. Toyota is known for its unrelenting ability to produce reliable cars. What about if I say the word 'Volvo', what is the first thing that comes to your mind? How about 'safety'? When Virgin Airlines came into the market in Australia, they were known as the 'cheaper' alternative. Now they have changed their brand promise to being the most 'revolutionary' airline.

How do you get your customers to buy from you more frequently? First, you must understand their buying patterns with you. You can usually obtain this information from your accounting system by printing a 'Sales by customer by month' report. I don't think there are many accounting systems on the market that would not provide you with this information. This will show you quite clearly how many times and when customers buy your products and services. Once you take the time to review and understand this, you can then determine appropriate strategies to assist your customers to buy your existing and new products and services more frequently. It may also suggest clues as to what your brand word ought to be if you haven't established an effective one already.

SUCCESS TIP
Understand what, when and how often your existing customers currently buy from you. This information provides you with the basis to have a conversation with your customer as to how to better service them. This information will unearth further opportunities to provide your products and services more regularly to them.

Creating the Sales and
Marketing Budget Model

Earlier in this chapter, I spoke of the model that I created for business owners that links your sales and marketing implementation plan to your financial budget. The model is simple and combines all of the knowledge presented above.

All you need to develop this hugely effective twelve-month budget is an Excel spreadsheet. How great is that? I told you I like to keep things simple.

To create your budget, there are eight steps that provide the best path to successfully set up this model.

Each step is detailed on the following pages.

Step One:

From your accounting software package, export your prior year's profit and loss statement broken down by month into your preferred spreadsheet package. (Obviously, if you are a start-up, you will not have this information, so you will have to create a budget from scratch.) This forms the summary page of your budgeted profit and loss.

Step Two:

Once you have created this summary page, you need to create a new sheet headed 'Sales'. This spreadsheet page combines all of the sales and marketing strategies listed above. We use Jay Abraham's three ways to grow your business as the foundation for the structure of this sheet.

Step Three:

From your accounting software, export the sales by customer by month report, and import it to the Sales Sheet that you created in Step Two. This provides you with the customer list of who purchased your products and services and when they purchased them. This information forms part of the low-hanging fruit that we've discussed so far.

This spreadsheet also provides you with what you need to know about your retention rate, since you can assess from the list whether the customers who bought from you last year are still likely to buy from you in the budgeted forecast year.

Flag the customers who have not bought from you for a while, as these customers may no longer be customers. If you are unsure if they are actually going to buy from you in the future, part of your sales and marketing strategy will now be to find out that information. Get your salespeople to contact these customers and have a meeting. The purpose of this meeting will be to determine if they will be purchasing and when. If they will not be purchasing and therefore no longer want to be your customer, use that time to find out why they left. You can also use that meeting to resurrect the relationship if possible.

The second sales and marketing activity that can be generated from this report is to assess the frequency that customers purchase from you. At a glance, you'll know how many times and when each customer purchased from you. Some accounting software packages also provide you with the data on what products or services they actually purchased. It is more likely that you obtained this information from your CRM program. Remember that one of the strategies was to increase the frequency in which your customers buy from you. If your customers are currently purchasing from you five times a year, then you need to determine a strategy to get them to purchase from you more times per year. Sell them your existing products more often or develop and sell new products resulting in an increased frequency of purchase. I find the easiest way to do this is to have a meeting with your customers to better understand their business. You may find the opportunity to assist them whilst increasing the need for your product at the same time. This is a bit of a double whammy for you, as you have first demonstrated to your customer that you understand their business, so they instantly know that you think and care for their business, and you have demonstrated your level of expertise. As a result, you will build trust and sell more products and services. Pretty simple, eh?

The cool part about this is that whilst it provides you with an activity plan, it also provides you with a greater ability to estimate what sales may be generated from each customer over the next twelve months. So it puts some science and substance behind your forecasted budget.

From one sheet you can start to estimate and project the impact of price increases, frequency of purchase increases and where the opportunities lie in selling new products. All this information is given on top of the fact that the spreadsheet provides you with an actual, rather than an estimate, of your retention rate.

We have now effectively provided you with the growth strategy to help you increase your frequency and average value per sale all in one sheet. Now some of you may still struggle with this exercise because you are still predicting the future and outcomes of meetings that you have not held. I get this, but at least if you predict the future, it is more likely to come true than if you don't, because completing this task will drive your monthly activity. Make sure that you are estimating the revenue that you will receive from each customer each month. One of Ron Baker's favourite quotes (founder of the VeraSage Institute and a LinkedIn Influencer) is, 'It is better to be approximately right, rather than precisely wrong.'

Hopefully by now you're seeing why the power of a budget is not only in providing you with the map but also with a goal. The specific goal then allows you every month to assess if you have achieved or not achieved the goal, that is, the budget variance. Now instead of saying either we did or did not achieve budget, you will know what activity worked and what did not work. You won't need to arbitrarily assess performance as now you can specifically assess performance based on activity. This will form part of your sales department's KPIs, so there is alignment with your salespeople's goals and your overall business revenue goals.

Step Four:

Now it's all about growing your customer base. So this is where you can project the sales based on the number of estimated leads and the conversion of those leads into customers. Whilst this projection can be arbitrary, once again, we can put some science and substance around the numbers.

The first thing to do is list all of the prospects you would like to target if known. Then you need to predict what sort of level of spending and how frequently they may buy from you and when to populate your budget each month. This is, once again, a very difficult thing to do because you are predicting the future based on assumption. Once again, I encourage you to do the best you can. Because if you have a plan, and there is activity arising from your plan, you are more likely to achieve it. It will also provide your salespeople with the infrastructure, discipline and direction they need to achieve their targets.

Once you have exhausted your known targets, you then need to list all of your centres of influence. What are centres of influence? Centres of influence are people who know your ideal customer and have influence over their buying decisions. So if they recommend your services to their contacts, those contacts are more likely to buy from you. These prospects are what are known as 'warm leads'. List these people down, and attempt to predict how many new customers you would like to convert from them. You will no doubt have to determine strategies to provide incentives for these centres of influence to be motivated enough to refer customers to you.

Finally, we need to rely on sales and marketing strategies to generate leads to your business. For businesses that have a mature trading history, there will be a track record of leads and conversion rates that have been established. Now you need to determine what marketing activity will be completed for the new financial year and the estimated number of leads that will be generated from this activity. Obviously, the goal is to generate more quality targeted leads. Each month there should be a budget of the number of leads the business should generate. Every month there should also be a number of conversions from prospects to customers to achieve.

Step Five:

Step Four drives all of this activity, which will provide an estimated sales figure per month for the next twelve months. This monthly figure should then be linked back to the sales figure on the summary profit and loss page. This provides empirical comparison data, which is foundational to success.

Step Six:

The complexity of determining your cost of sales and your gross profit is influenced by whether you sell products or services. Many non-accountants do not really understand the terms cost of sales and gross profit. They generally are confused whether an expense is an overhead expense or a cost of sale. Here's the simplest way to explain it: if the expense is only incurred due to the sale of the product or service, then it is a cost of sale and not an overhead. Overhead expenses will occur in isolation to the sale, for example, rent, utilities, licence fees, accounting fees, etc. These are the costs of keeping the business doors open, so to speak. The distinction is important for a number of reasons. It allows you to benchmark your business in the industry you operate to determine if you are performing well against your competitors. It also assists in determining your break-even point.

Now, what's the break-even point, and how do you calculate it? To break even means that you neither make a profit or a loss—that is, your profit is zero. The purpose of calculating your break-even point is to determine the level of sales you are required to achieve for the profit to be zero. To calculate the break-even sales, you take the overhead expenses and divide it by the gross profit margin. This equates to your break-even sales figure. To calculate your gross profit margin, you divide your gross profit into your total sales.

We will cover in more depth the concept of working capital and the time and cost of resources required to achieve the budgeted sales in Chapter 6. We explain how to turn a budgeted profit and loss into a cash flow forecast.

For the purposes of budgeting, you need to determine the appropriate gross profit margin based on a percentage of cost of sales.

Step Seven:

Now we need to determine the overhead costs required to support the business and achieve the sales budget. This includes determining what infrastructure and resources are required in the business to ensure that the business can achieve the sales forecast.

Overheads are referred to as fixed costs. These costs by their nature are fixed and not variable based on the level of sales. Generally, these costs are known within a high degree of certainty. Therefore, it is a lot easier to predict future expenses as compared to sales and cost of sales.

A tip for you when forecasting your fixed overhead is to make sure, where possible, you do not merely take the total estimated expenditure for the year and divide by twelve to get the monthly figure. If you know the pattern of expenditure, then ensure that this is reflected in your budget summary page so each month has the appropriate expense. This reduces the requirement to explain the variance each month against the budgeted figure.

In most cases where a business employs staff, I recommend that a separate sheet be set up for wages. This sheet should include all of the staff wages broken down between departments. It should also include predicted salary increases and commission structure based on sales. The reason it should be broken down into departments is that some of the wages may be included as a cost of sales, rather than an overhead, so they can be linked to the summary profit and loss page in the appropriate section.

Once you have completed this step, you should have determined your monthly overhead expenditure for the business.

Step Eight:

By completing steps one to seven, you should have determined your overall profit or loss for the business for the next twelve months. The time has come to review the total budgeted profit or loss to determine if it is an acceptable return on investment for the owners. Probably a better measure is whether it is an acceptable return on effort. In other words, is all the forecasted effort worth the result of the profit? Work backwards to determine what the sales, cost of sales and overheads need to be to achieve the appropriate level of profit. Remember, I referred to this as the top-down, bottom-up process of determining the budget. Steps one to seven complete the top-down approach; if you are not happy with the result, then you should complete the bottom-up process.

Monthly Budget Review and Accountability

Can you see the power of putting together and integrating your sales and marketing plan with your budget? Reviewing how you went against the budget on a monthly basis to see if you achieved your numbers also provides enormous benefits. Now you can confidently explain the variance based on specific activities and not arbitrary numbers alone.

In summary, if you start to know your numbers, or if you want to define your numbers better, you must focus on the parameters. If you can break your sales forecast into the categories listed above, you are more likely to achieve the result and be more targeted in the process. Do not leave things to chance.

The budget forms a very significant part of the map. I believe that it is core to the map, as it becomes the window through which you can see the results of the strategy.

Chapter 5

ARE WE ON TRACK?

Financial Information

Something interesting happened at one of my monthly customer director's meetings. The purpose of the meeting was to create the following year budget. This particular customer, a husband and wife team, ran a construction business that had been in operation for over five years. As I had only recently started working with this business, they had not been through a full twelve-month cycle with me consulting and advising them. It was the first time that I had the opportunity to set a budget with them. From our first meeting it was clear that they did not have a defined budget and didn't know the numbers in their business. For the record, as I have said before, when business owners do not know their numbers, I get it. They haven't been provided with proper support and advice from their accountants and advisors, and it's impacting their business decisions and stagnating their success.

After our initial meeting, I reviewed their accounting data file and prepared a budget template based on the eight steps outlined in Chapter 4. I will let you in on a secret—I usually do not prepare these budgets myself, because it is no longer an effective use of my time. The team I work with have been trained on how to complete it for businesses. However, as happens in any business, a calamity occurred and required me to take on this task on this particular day. So I did. Also, I really enjoyed getting back on the tools and preparing a budget spreadsheet, but that can be between you and me. Not only because as an accountant you get a sense of achievement when you create something that is going to change the way a business owner thinks about their business, but also I was relieved that I still had the skills. (It IS like riding a bike, as they say.) Finally, the great part was I used the instructions set out in Chapter 4 as a test to see if my knowledge translates, and it does. (Phew!)

Just as I started to present my information and findings for the business, I was stopped by one of the business owners. She indicated that it was all good and well to talk about the budget, but as a team, they did not know which jobs were profitable and whether they had the capacity to complete those jobs. You could really sense the confusion, frustration and uneasiness in their voices and on their faces. So I took a new approach as I provided this information.

My first question to these business owners was to ask what different types of construction they offered. They replied that there were two distinct types. So we went through an exercise on how they priced the jobs. From this exercise it was evident that they priced on a 'cost plus' basis to obtain the selling price. So their business was heavily reliant on gross profit margin to drive profit. Once we established the margin for each job from an estimate perspective, I then went through what the actual costs of sales were for each of these two distinct jobs to obtain the true gross profit margin. Interestingly enough, one job had a gross profit margin of 43% and the other had a gross profit margin of 24%. What does gross profit margin mean again? It is the profit left after you subtract the direct selling costs on the job. (Refer back to page 89 in Chapter 4 if you need further revision.)

It quickly became obvious that this construction business needed to concentrate on the jobs that provided the highest gross profit margin. However, it is not always as simple as this because, as you might guess after reading the first four chapters of this book, the owners need to know how much each job was worth (in terms of revenue generated) and the direct costs involved to produce a profitable result. Calculating the gross profit margin alone is not enough. The volume of transactions is important, because that will influence the capacity of the business. In this situation, we discovered that it took the same amount of time and required the same amount of resources to do both kinds of construction, so it was more profitable to complete the jobs with the higher margin.

SUCCESS TIP
Determine the profitability of each job or product in your business.

I could then see the relief on their faces as they started to get answers to the questions that had plagued them for years. So in one hour with a spreadsheet, we solved their two biggest questions: What jobs should we undertake and what profit do these jobs return? And, do we do more of these jobs to make a profit? This meant that the next step was to review the numbers based on their capacity. The calculation showed that they could take on approximately 130 jobs per year, or around eleven per month. How did I work this out so quickly? Well, in the words of Mike and Mal Leyland, the Leyland Brothers, 'I am glad you asked.' (Sorry to anyone reading this born after 1990. They are kind of like Steve Irwin on sedatives.) I asked, 'What is the resource that is required on each job that will limit each job from being completed without it?' The answer: Their excavator.

Each job required this machine for the work to be completed. It was usually used for three and a half days per job, so based on a forty-five-week year (forty-five weeks is used as a conservative period which presents fifty-two weeks in a year, less annual leave, sick leave, public holidays and other unaccounted for downtime), this meant that the maximum number of jobs the excavator could complete was sixty-four per year. This business had two excavators, which meant they could complete a maximum of 128 jobs per year.

Now that the business owners knew that they had a limited capacity of jobs they could complete, based on their resources, they gained a huge sense of relief. Their main problem was not the volume of work they had available to them, it was how to work smarter. Knowing their capacity meant that they could concentrate on the higher margin work, and they knew they could supply the demand available. The best part of this conversation with the customer was that they discovered that they could do less work and earn more money. This resulted in an increase to their estimated profit by $250,000. Historically, to achieve this profit, they would need three excavators working, and they personally worked ridiculous hours to achieve it.

Then we worked on how they were going to go after these jobs from a sales and marketing perspective. First, I reviewed their customer list to see who had bought from them in consecutive years. The reason why I did not work out how many customers they have is because this company is predominantly a transactional business (see Chapter 4, 'Budgeting'). However, there is an opportunity to turn even a construction company into a relationship business. We then worked out the type of business that could refer the type of work they wanted which is where there were centres of influence. Finally, we reviewed how many leads they needed to obtain to achieve three jobs per week. At the time, the business owners were quoting on 310 opportunities per year. These quotes converted to 130 sales, which meant that the sales conversion rate was 42%.

We then estimated that the business owners could increase their conversion percentage if they filtered the leads coming into the business and only quoted on the work that resulted in the higher gross profit. When I asked them if that sounded like a great idea, the answer was a resounding 'Yes'! So their new sales conversion percentage is 50%, which now means that they only need to quote 260 times, not 310. What does all this mean? Well, the business owners now can call me up to play golf more often. (Not that I have time to play golf with a young family!)

> **SUCCESS TIP**
> Your sales and marketing plan to attract new customers should be focused on the most profitable goods or services that you sell.

In two hours we worked out the budget, the KPIs and the focus of the business owners with one spreadsheet as the tool. Pretty cool, eh? I went home that night feeling happy, so I thought that I would share this story with you. What was even better was how grateful the customers were about this experience; they no longer needed to work the very long hours that they had previously been operating the business, and they had increased their bottom line by simply better understanding the data that they already had, but had not previously used. It also meant that they had the confidence to continue to review and refine the data and how they operated their business, because they now knew what to look for.

This is a common example about how to know when you are on track. This team was not on track prior to the meeting, but now they have the strategy and the implementation plan to drive significant results to the bottom line. Having said this, it is not over yet for these guys. When they are at capacity again, I will recommend purchasing a third excavator, which will potentially drive a further $500,000 to their bottom line. We will see below what financial information we need to review to ensure that you are keeping on track. For this example, the three KPIs, or smart numbers that they needed to keep track of were:

1. The gross profit margin
2. Leads generated on their preferred jobs
3. Conversion of leads

They just had to focus on these numbers for the next three months to see serious results.

Are you on track with your financial information?

Now that you have prepared the map and you have started your journey, we need to keep watch for road signs to ensure that we are on the right road. Also, because the destination can be a long way from the starting point, we need to have milestones, which represent smaller goals along the way. These goals are like townships you pass along the way to your ultimate destination.

Why is it so important to have milestones? Milestones assist for two reasons. One is that they signify that you are on track and the other is that they provide the momentum to continue on. Remember in Chapter 1 when we spoke about the importance of mindset? Being in business is not a sprint. It is a marathon. We need wins along the way to ensure that we maintain focus and keep the momentum to continue on. Business is tough, so anything that you can do to keep your mindset focused and strong is required to prevent distractions and poor motivation, which leads to poor performance and failure.

Many times I've seen business owners struggle and want to give up because they can't see the destination. My job is sensing whether they need a pat on the back or a slap (metaphorically speaking). When I meet with customers on a monthly basis to review their performance and determine if they are on track with their strategy, I often get a sense of their mental state. Sometimes they need a good kick up the bum, because they are being lazy and not focusing on what they should. Other times they need empathy, support and guidance to push them through the hard times, to keep them focused on the journey and to ensure they get to the finish line.

SUCCESS TIP
Make sure that you are very clear on the destination. Then write a list of the milestones along the way that will get you to that destination.

You may have heard the statement, 'What you can't measure you can't manage.' Well, this is one of my main mantras. Not because I am an accountant, but because I see the benefit to this in keeping you on track with your mindset. Unfortunately, humans are more motivated to avoid pain than to embrace it. Being in business can be painful and needs to be embraced. Setting milestones can assist with managing your mindset. How do we know if we are moving if we don't know the starting point, the end point and the measure along the way? Moving towards a goal gives you a sense of achievement and therefore provides the continual momentum to keep going. Largely the reason why people give up is because they don't sense forward movement, and what they see is a long, difficult road ahead. Their confidence plummets, and they wonder if they can actually achieve their goals. Soon, the motivation to continue on ends. Once you lose that motivation, it is hard to find it again.

Now you know the importance of measurement, we need to know what to measure. There are two distinct components that we need to measure in a business: one is performance and the other is position. In the accounting world, the profit and loss statement is a measure of performance over a period of time, and the balance sheet measures the financial position of the business at a given point in time. As I indicated in the last chapter, using a balance sheet and a profit and loss statement to assess your business performance is not enough. I acknowledge that you can get a lot of information about a business from these reports; however, we need to drill down to look behind these numbers to explain what is really going on in the business.

SUCCESS TIP
Measure everything and then monitor the progress towards the goal.

Let me show you what we get from these global reports based on a business' balance sheet and profit and loss statement and then what specific measures we need to look at to determine what is going on behind these numbers.

Now, before we get started, my goal is not to turn you into accountants with this information. My goal is to provide you with the critical information you need to make informed decisions about your business. I will focus on the information that is easily understandable and provides you with great insight. Recently, I had an interesting conversation with a business owner about his business. He said that business is fundamentally boring. I asked him to elaborate on this point. He said that he thought that business would be more exciting and interesting, but it isn't what he thought it would be. He mentioned that all the things that I had taught him about, in reality, are boring (no disrespect intended). It can be boring because there is such a prescribed formula about what to do and how to do it. You may think that I might have been a little offended with these comments, but in this situation I was extremely pleased. I had finally gotten through.

Let me explain. When I first met this business owner and started working with him, he acted like a bit of a rock star. His business was growing fast, and he had money in the bank and started to get seriously distracted by going off on tangents. Twelve months later, he had built this business but was broke. This was because he did not build the business on strong fundamentals, and what he thought was the financial position of the business wasn't. He now had to work his way out of a difficult financial situation. In that meeting he said 'should have' and 'why didn't I' more often than I'd ever heard before. He said he botched everything by ignoring advice to put KPIs in place for his team to hold them accountable and measure their performance. In this meeting we realised that he had to let go of four people in his business because he could not afford to keep them. Because he's a really nice bloke, he found this process excruciating.

This business owner learnt a very difficult lesson, and it's one he'll never forget. At times, business owners need to act on the boring stuff if they want long-term success. It was unfortunate that he had to learn it the very hard way and hit rock bottom before he made the mindset changes he needed in relation to his attitude towards successfully operating a business.

SUCCESS TIP
Don't get ahead of yourself. Make sure that you really know your financial situation before making strategic growth decisions for your business.

Now do you understand why it's essential to be disciplined in business?

Profit and Loss KPIs

More of the boring stuff (for some). For those not familiar with the term, a profit and loss statement is made up of three sections: income, cost of sales and overhead expenses. We have already covered how critical KPIs are to sales in setting the budget. Knowing your leads, conversion of prospects to new customers, average transaction per sale and the number of times the customer purchases from you will explain the variance between the budgeted versus actual sales income. I recommend that you review your numbers monthly by comparing monthly and year-to-date performance against last year, budget and actual.

The most important item to note about cost of sales is tracking the margin. That is, sales less cost of sales equal gross profit. The gross profit margin is calculated by dividing the gross profit into sales. We set this margin when completing the budget, so once again it is all about ensuring that you review your margins monthly.

However, this information alone will not assist you in determining the reason for the variance. You will need to drill down further to understand why there possibly is a variance. How you do this will depend on the business you operate. If you operate predominantly a service-based business, you may want to track the profit on each job. Every accounting system I have used has the capacity to keep track of the profit for each job. That will tell you where the variances come from. If your business predominantly sells products, then your inventory system will determine the margin that you are obtaining on each stock item. If you don't use an inventory system, then I suggest you do so, because there are plenty on the market that are relativity low-cost or are embedded into your accounting system. Without this extra information, you can only guess why there is a variance to your margin.

This is why you need to produce gross profit reports on each product or job to see where you are making and losing money specifically in each area of your business.

Finally, you need to keep track of your overhead expense. This is as simple as monitoring your expenditures against your budget to ensure that you are on track. If there is a variance, you can drill down into your transactions to determine an explanation.

I know that some of you will look at this and go, 'Wow! That is not rocket science. It's actually quite simple.' But a majority of businesses are not run with these numbers. Sure, most people know that businesses ought to be run this way, and the reason that they don't is because they either don't know how or don't allocate enough time to the process.

Balance Sheet KPIs

A balance sheet is made up of assets, liabilities and equity. Every month that I conduct a customer review, I look at the balance sheet predominantly for one purpose and that is cash. Does the business have enough cash to meet all of its obligations?

If you have been in business for a while, no doubt you have had the question, 'Why don't I have any cash when I made a profit?' We will speak about this further in Chapter 6. With regard to the measures, I am looking at whether the business has sufficient liquidity for the working capital requirements of the business. The best measure to quickly check the health of the cash position of the business is to calculate the liquidity ratio. The liquidity ratio determines the coverage of liquid assets to short-term debt.

Liquid assets are cash or assets that can be turned into cash in a short period, like debtors. Short-term debt is the liabilities in the business that have to be paid within a short period of time, for example, usually up to three months, which include trade creditors and statutory obligations (goods and services tax, pay-as-you-go withholding, payroll tax, super, etc.).

Here is the formula:

$$\frac{\text{Liquid Assets (Cash at Bank and Debtors)}}{\text{Short-Term Debts (Trade Creditors and Statutory Obligations)}}$$

Ratios, on their own, are meaningless unless you understand how to interpret the result. Here is my rule of thumb interpretation. To be able to pay your debts, you need to have a result greater than 1. This means that you have more liquid assets than short-term debts. If you have a number less than one, you need to have a plan to increase this to greater than one, otherwise you can be deemed to be insolvent trading. If you are trading the business whilst insolvent, you as the director can be held personally liable for any debts that you incur once the business is insolvent.

When I review liquidity ratios, I usually know how much sleep a business owner is getting. If you have a ratio less than 1, you are not getting very much sleep at all, because you are worrying about how you are going to pay wages and stop the Australian Taxation Office from liquidating your business. If you have a ratio of between 1 and 1.5 times, you will be getting to sleep, but more often than not waking up at 3:00 a.m. worrying how you are going to manage your cash flow because things are tight. Once you get beyond 1.5 times to 2 times, cash still needs to be monitored on a weekly basis, but it is not usually keeping you awake. Once you are above 2 times, you really don't have to worry about cash other than monitor it for changes on a monthly basis. This means that you have twice the amount of cash assets to cover short-term debts, so the timing of when you receive payment from your debtors does not have to be closely monitored to pay your short-term debts.

Not having enough cash is a massive problem, but having too much cash is not ideal either, because it means that you may have a lazy balance sheet. If the cash is sitting in your business, it may be exposed from an asset protection perspective and will not be providing a sufficient return.

The other indicator that I use from these reports is the average debtor days. This indicator measures the average number of days it takes from the date the invoice is generated to the time the money is collected from the customer. The longer the time it takes, the more working capital is required to fund the business. We explain this further in Chapter 6. For the purposes of the indicator, it is healthy to determine the liquidity in the business. Once we assess this macro indicator, we then drill down into the actual accounts receivable list to find out which customers are not paying inside of terms.

Here is the formula:

$$\frac{\text{Debtors}}{\text{Year-to-Date Sales}} \quad X \quad \text{Year-to-Date Days}$$

The number of days it takes to collect from your customers will depend on the business. This measure is not necessary for businesses that operate on a cash basis at the time of sale. It is relevant when a business provides terms with regards to their payments, for example, seven, fourteen, twenty-one or thirty days are the most common. If your average debtor days are the same or better than your terms, then you are doing very well, and we do not consider this to be an issue. If your average debtor days are significantly more than your terms, then this will be an area to focus on. In summary, the longer the number of days it takes to collect the debts, the more money you need to fund your business until you collect your debts. The average number of days it takes to collect your debts in Australia is forty-five. I heard a statistic once—and I'm not sure that it is true, but it sounds logical—that the average number of days it takes to collect from customers in Germany is three days. Culturally, it's seen as a poor reflection on your business if you take longer than three days to pay your debts. In Australia, my observation has been that businesses tend to pay on the last day. But if everyone paid immediately, then you could pay everyone else immediately; often the reason you pay late is because you are also awaiting payment. So it becomes a self-repeating cycle. This is hugely frustrating for small business owners. From my experience, the biggest culprits of longer payment terms are large businesses. They dictate payment terms based on what they want to do (some may suggest that the businesses are inefficient so this drags out these terms). Effectively, these large businesses force the longer payment cycle in Australia. The additional frustration is that these larger institutions are often the ones that can afford to pay earlier but they don't. Ultimately the SMEs end up carrying the strain. Maybe this is something that you could consider as a differentiator in your business – paying in the short term?

Another measure that we use as macro indicators of the health of the business are average stock turnover or average work in progress (WIP) depending on whether you sell goods or services. We also discuss this idea further in Chapter 6.

Efficiency Reporting

Every business needs to assess their levels of resourcing and efficiency. Why? Because this is critical to meeting and exceeding your customer's expectations by delivering your goods and services. And that is where you will make or lose money.

In Chapter 4 there was commentary about the need to ensure that you have sufficient resources to support the sales budget. The calculated resources are based on the assumption that your resources will be efficient and effective. In a manufacturing sense, it will be measured by the output of the machine, but how do we measure people's output? If you work in a service-based business where you effectively sell a person's knowledge and ability, like accounting, mostly timesheets are used to determine performance. However, if you don't run an operation where timesheets are used and you would like to determine a measure of performance, you can consider using a measure such as the average hourly recovery rate of your employees.

In your service-based business, you will have people who deliver the services and charge for their time effectively, and you will have people who provide support which is the administration staff. First, you need to work out the total time a person is available to charge. In most professional businesses, this will be 1,800 hours (8 hours per day x 5 days x 45 weeks in a year). In case you missed this in Chapter 5, why do we use forty-five weeks when there are fifty-two? This is due to taking into consideration annual leave, sick leave, public holidays and a further week of downtime. We then determine the percentage of available time to complete work for customers. Usually this is a percentage between 50% and 90%. The reason it is not 100% is because there is always time that people have in their day that will not be charged to completing customer work. If you then divide the available chargeable hours into the total revenue, you will produce an average dollar charged per hour. This is an interesting number because it is the real sale price for each hour that you have available to charge. While advocates of *Implementing Value Pricing* would suggest that we don't equate dollars to hours, for some businesses it is necessary to start somewhere until you know how to do it better.

Recently, I completed this exercise with a customer who operates an IT support service business. When we calculated the average hourly recovery across his professional team (or how much money his staff members brought into the company for each available hour they could charge to a customer), it came out to $30 per hour. The business owner was shocked and stated that it was very much less than expected. Particularly, when you think about what is required to become an IT expert, the years of study and the complexity of operating this type of business, $30 per hour seemed low. The business owner charges his professional staff out at between $150 per hour and $225 per hour plus GST.

The next question I had for the customer was: 'Why is this rate per hour low and how can we increase it?' As there were a number of possible reasons, further investigation was required to determine the actual reason this was occurring in his business. The investigation uncovered a combination of problems. First, the business was charging a monthly fixed fee based on providing a certain level of service to their customers. To calculate the monthly fee for the customer, the business owner estimated that they would need to provide a certain number of hours to complete this service. When we did the analysis on each individual job, we discovered that it took two to three times longer to provide the service as compared to what was originally estimated in the fixed price. In a professional services business, this is known as a write-off. So they had a significant write-off problem. They also underused capacity. The analysis indicated that of the available professional time to be charged to customers, they were only at 60% capacity. In this case they had more resources than there was demand for based on the number of customers that they had.

Now we agree that service providers who traditionally charge an hourly rate need to stop doing this and instead, charge a fee based on the value of the outcome to the customer. The price should be dictated up front, based on a fair price for the job. Because the provision of services is based on people power, then we must ensure that the return on the staff member's time is profitable. This customer had a twofold charging issue: he was underestimating how long it would take his people to complete the tasks, and his people did not know how long they had to complete each task. So we had to work on both issues. I am pleased to say that after working on these two issues, the average hourly recovery rate for this business is up to $138. Our goal is to get it to over $175 per hour, and we are now well on our way.

How did we do it? The short answer is that we went back and renegotiated service level agreements with their customers to ensure that the service provided was commensurate with the requirements of the customer. We found that the resources team was providing services outside the scope of the original fixed price agreement, so we factored variations either into the service level agreement to increase the fixed price, or we stated that any work completed outside the service level agreement would be charged at an hourly rate. Then we sat down with the team to discuss the issue of over-servicing and how to operate more efficiently on jobs. The main reason for the inefficiency was that the team was not aware of the budget and how to monitor their time. They also were not fully aware of the scope of work to be undertaken that was included in the original fixed price agreement.

This showed that a large part of the issue was lack of communication and information. As such, we installed a full end-to-end IT support-specific system that monitored both the team's performance and the performance of the business in delivering to their customers. Of course, this is the short answer; there were lots of other strategies implemented and problems encountered along the way in fixing the issue, but those were the main issues. I am also pleased to report that this business now has very happy customers and is much more profitable than before. So the business owner is very happy too.

Financial Information

There are three distinct staff members you need in your accounting department: a bookkeeper, a management accountant and a chief financial officer (CFO). Most SMEs do not have the luxury of having all three experts. They generally have a bookkeeper who, if she is good, will try to complete all of the management accounting tasks.

The reason the SMEs do not have this resource is that they are not of the size to justify having full-time staff members to assist. Moreover, trying to access these people on a part-time basis is difficult. Knowing this gap exists in the marketplace, we have developed an outsourced accounting function and a virtual CFO service for our customers. This service gets them the information they need to make strategic business decisions based on sound financial information.

Based on over ten years of experience providing management financial reports to SMEs, we have developed a pack of financial information that provides a window on the financial status and performance of the business each month.

On one page, we advise the monthly performance against budget, the year-to-date performance against the budget, the forecast for the rest of the year and the projected profit at the end of the year. On one page you know your current performance, your recent performance, what you need to achieve for the rest of the year and what the result will be at the end of the year if you achieve it. Pretty cool, eh? We developed this model over ten years ago, and the good news for you is that the modern accounting software packages produce this information as part of their reporting process, so you have even greater access to it than ever before. Now the trick is in interpreting the information. This is where you need a good accountant/advisor to assist with the inter-pretation of the information to educate you on the result.

The list of reports that you should review monthly is:

- Profit and Loss Statement (Budget vs. Actual for Month and Year-to-Date)

- Balance Sheet (showing movements from prior month to current month)

- Cash Flow Forecast

- Job/Product Profit and Loss

- Accounts Receivable

- Accounts Payable

- KPI Reporting against Targets

The above are the basic reports that we encourage business owners to focus on. We suggest that each business reports on information that will assist with knowing if their business is on track through specific KPI reporting tailored to their business needs.

From our experience, just doing the above goes a long way compared to what most business owners are currently producing.

SUCCESS TIP
Every goal should be measurable and every measure should have a desired outcome. Once established, you need to continually monitor your numbers against the progress of the goal.

Chapter 6

HOW MUCH ROAD CAN WE TRAVEL ON?

Cash Flow

You made a profit but you have no cash in the bank! How does that work? I get this question at least once a week. The other statement I regularly hear is that the business owner feels like all he does is pay tax and never gets ahead. By the way, we all feel like that sometimes: we pay tax, and every time we get cash in the bank, we have to pay tax and out it goes. If this sounds like you, then you are going to get a lot out of this chapter. There is a way to plan so you know exactly how much cash you should have at the end of every month forecasted over a twelve-month period.

In Chapter 4, we explained how to effectively budget for a profit. Part of the budgeting process is to budget for sufficient cash reserves to sustain the business and the business owner's desired lifestyle. You may have worked out while reading this book that I like to do things fast when it comes to planning and implementing, because business owners are time-poor. Fortunately, there is a quick and easy way to take a budgeted profit and loss and turn it into a forecasted cash flow statement. Before I tell you how, let me tell you that I don't like the concept of cash flow; I like cash retention. 'Cash flow' means that money is coming in and going out again; I prefer to focus on the cash that gets retained in your business.

How would you like to know how much cash you should have in your bank account at the end of each month for the next twelve months? Most of you would say, 'I can't achieve this because my business is too unpredictable.' Whilst that may be true, at least we can attempt to predict it based on assumptions. Remember, we put further science behind achieving your budgeted profit, so there is a greater chance that your future will turn up because you know the activities that have to be completed in order for the result to arrive. What we will do now is turn that forecasted profit and loss budget into a cash flow forecast.

Before we do, let me address the question of why profit does not equal cash. There are two major reasons for this. One is that the flow of cash is allocated according to certain criteria. The net flow of cash in and cash out may not be the exact same number as the 'revenue in' and 'expenses out' number as seen on your profit and loss statement.

Second, most businesses record their transactions using the accruals accounting method rather than the cash accounting method.

Let's look more closely at each of these.

The first reason, if you look at your bank account, there will be a series of transactions that go in and out leaving a balance. Bookkeeping is all about recording each transaction in your business and organising it into a readable form, resulting in the production of a profit and loss statement and a balance sheet. As we've already seen, there is also a lot of other information that we can obtain from the recording of transactions, but for the purposes of this conversation, we are going to concentrate on the profit and loss statement and balance sheet. Now before your eyes start to glaze over, there is a point to telling you this. I know that it's fairly basic, but it is amazing how many times I have explained these concepts this way, and people have thanked me because it all makes sense now. I even explain this to graduate accountants that we employ because universities are great at teaching theory and not practice. I know this because I've employed multiple graduates every year for the last ten years.

Some of these transactions are recorded in the profit and loss statement and some in the balance sheet. So it is implicit that the profit will not equal cash at the bank. The other item to note is that accounting is based on what is known as the double entry system. Double entry means that every transaction must have two sides, a debit side and a credit side. The result of the double entry accounting system is that the balance sheet always balances. Now most people could not care less about this information, but to accountants, this is their lifeblood. It takes a certain type of person to be an accountant. Here is an insight into their mind. When I hold graduate interviews, I ask the candidate about what has drawn them to accounting. Nearly every answer involves the following response: 'I like accounting because I like it when I balance the numbers.' They like the certainty of the answer and enjoy getting the answer right. See? I told you it takes a certain type of person to like accounting. Personally, I felt the same way when I started in the profession. My reasons for staying in the profession are oh-so-different now, as you may have surmised from the experiences I have shared in this book.

In getting back to recording transactions in the bank account into either the profit and loss statement or balance sheet, I will now indicate what goes where. There is still a point to this, which when you understand, you will never ask the question as to, 'Where did my cash go when I made a profit?' On the credit side of the bank statement is all the money coming into the business and on the debit side of the bank statement is all the money going out. It is recorded on the opposite side of the ledger in your accounts because you are the bank's creditor. They are holding money on your behalf if there is cash in the bank.

Money coming into the business may be in the form of income, which would go into the profit and loss statement, or it may be due to money being loaned to the business, in which case it is not income, but will be recorded as a loan in the balance sheet. On the debit side of the bank statement, money going out may be to pay expenses, which would be recorded in your profit and loss statement, or it may be to purchase an asset, in which case it's not an expense, it is an asset purchase, and will be recorded as an asset in the balance sheet. Money going out of the bank account may also be repaying a liability like a loan, so this would not affect the profit and loss statement of the business; however, it definitely affects the cash flow of the business.

Assets often affect the profit and loss statement of a business. Usually assets are 'written off' or depreciated over the life of the asset (as determined by accounting standards). This effectively gradually reduces the dollar amount of the asset on the balance sheet, and because of that double entry system there needs to be a balancing entry. That entry is an expense in the profit and loss statement. This reduces the profit of the business. However, this is commonly known in accounting circles as a non-cash business transaction, because it affects profit, but not the flow of cash. Seeing the point now? Accounting can be complex; however, understanding some of the basics will be a huge plus to your business in the long term.

Moving on to the second main reason why profit does not equal cash, which is due to the accrual accounting method. The accrual accounting method is about recording transactions when there is an obligation to receive or pay money, not when it is actually paid. (The purist accounting academics just had a heart attack or rolled over in their grave with this explanation. Apologies to my accounting forefathers.) The best way to explain this is to use an example. When you have completed a service or sold some goods, you create an invoice. If you provide payment terms (so the customer is not required to pay you on the spot), then it is appropriate to use the accruals accounting method. Because a sale has been made, you want to record this sale in your accounts. But because you have not received the money yet, you need to record a debtor in the balance sheet. So this sale will increase your profit but will not increase your bank account until the customer pays. At this point of the explanation, most people start to go, 'Ah, now I get it!'

The same applies when you have to pay a supplier for goods or services that your business engages. You may have received the benefits of the services or the goods but are not required to pay for them immediately because you have negotiated terms with the supplier. It is beneficial to record these obligations to pay so you are aware of what payments are required to be paid in the future in order to keep track of these before they hit your in tray. Take the same steps with the people who owe you money.

The lists that your accounting system produces with respect to suppliers that you owe and customers that owe you money are your accounts payable list and accounts receivable list respectively.

When is it appropriate to use the accruals or cash method for accounting purposes? If your customers are required to pay on the spot, then the cash accounting system may be the most relevant for you to use. If you predominantly invoice your customers, then the accrual accounting system may be the most relevant. Of course, check this with your advisor, as they will know best here.

If you made it to reading this, well done! Let's put all of this into action so you can better plan forecasting your cash.

To commence completing a cash flow forecast, we start with the budgeted profit and loss spreadsheet completed in Chapter 4. Then we add a new section at the bottom of the spreadsheet, the cash flow forecast. As indicated above, if we provide terms to our customers, we need to adjust the income to reflect those terms (that is, 7, 14, 21, 30 days). If you have been trading for a while, you will probably realise that not all of your customers adhere to your terms, and you may experience average debtor days to blow out to 60 or even 90 days. (This can be soul-destroying when you absolutely bust your gut to deliver a superior service, and your customers don't respect you enough to pay you on time.) The biggest number of debtor days I have encountered is 135 days. This business was waiting, on average, to be paid a third of the year. (That is ridiculous when they provided terms of 30 days. By the way, with strategies we implemented, I am pleased to say this business reduced its average debtor days to 40, and it is not over yet.)

The accrued income in the profit and loss budget is therefore split over the following months based on a level of the average collections. For example, if the average debtors' days are 60 days, then you would include 50% of the collections of the debtors in the following month and the balance in the month after. To clarify, consider the following example:

Profit and Loss Budget				
	July	August	September	October
Sales	$50,000	$100,000	$150,000	$100,000
Cash Flow Forecast				
Cash Inflow		$25,000	$75,000	$125,000

Looking at this example, you don't effectively collect all the cash from your sales in July and August until October.

The next step to convert your profit and loss budget into a cash flow forecast is to add back non-cash transactions, like depreciation and amortisation of assets. These entries in the profit and loss account are created by journal entry and do not affect cash. The actual purchase of the asset is what affects the cash flow.

If it is projected that the business is required to purchase an asset, like a computer, it should be included as a cash outflow in your cash flow forecast. However, if you are not anticipating paying cash for the asset and you are going to finance it, you need to include the finance as an inflow of money into your cash flow forecast.

If you negotiate terms with your suppliers, you will need to project when you are actually going to pay them in the same manner as your debtors as presented above.

If you sell goods rather than services, then you need to predict when you have to purchase and pay for stock working backwards from when you sell the stock. Generally you will need to have stock on hand ready to sell at the time the goods are sold and invoiced. If you purchase goods from overseas to potentially increase gross profit margin, this can be a cycle of three months.

I haven't mentioned the 'T' word for a couple of chapters. That's right, tax. Tax is often considered as a burden, but if you budget effectively for it, then it simply becomes transactional and a part of what you do in your usual budgeting. Business owners generally dislike tax more when it is unexpected. Some taxes are worse than others. A point that I have not previously mentioned is that the Goods and Services Tax (GST) is not included in the profit and loss. All transactions included in the profit and loss are net of the GST. The GST component is split and included in the balance sheet because the business is collecting the GST on behalf of the government. Therefore, it is an in-and-out transaction. What I mean by in-and-out is that you collect it, hold it on trust for the government and pay it on your Business Activity Statement (BAS) monthly or quarterly. The reason we get confused about this is that the money we collect from our debtors goes into our bank account.

So it hurts a lot when it comes time to pay the BAS. The only saving grace is that we do get a credit for the GST we pay in business, which is offset against the GST collected, so we only pay the difference on the BAS. We include the payment of the BAS; however, because it is an in-and-out transaction, it ultimately does not affect cash flow. It is a timing difference.

The other tax payable on the BAS or Instalment Activity Statement is Pay As You Go (PAYG) Withholding Tax, which is the tax deducted from wages. Usually the net wage is paid in one month and the PAYG Withholding Tax is paid in the following month. However, in a profit and loss statement, the gross is incurred in the same month. If wages remain fairly static from one month to the next, generally it is immaterial to make an adjustment for timing. So no adjustment is required from the budgeted profit and loss to the cash flow forecast.

The final major tax that needs to be taken into consideration that causes the most problems for most business owners is tax on the business profit (depending on the structure of the business will determine the type of tax required to be paid—again that specialist advice is required here). This is the tax that causes everyone grief. Why? It is complex to work out how much and when the tax will be due and payable. Let me explain how it works.

Tax on Profits

One of the biggest frustrations that send businesses to the wall is misunderstanding the timing and amount of tax payable. The reason being is that it is an obligation that sneaks up on most businesses. As discussed in Chapter 3, tax is paid on the profit of the business. If the business is set up as a company, then 30% of the profit is payable in tax. Now tax is really just another expense of the business. So why does it cause business so many issues? Largely, it is due to the tax not being payable immediately when profit is earned. Tax may not be payable for up to twenty-one months after a business commences or at minimum nine months after the end of the financial year when the profit is calculated. The time lag is the thing that causes the issue. But really the issue is that the business owner is not making a provision and budgeting for the tax.

There is also a massive sting in the tail for new businesses and businesses that are experiencing significant growth and expansion (I call it the tax double whammy). Let me explain by way of example.

Let's say there's a business set up as a corporate structure that in its first year, makes a profit of $100,000. Whilst we can estimate what the profit will be prior to the end of the year, we need to complete the year before we determine the actual profit. In Australia, the financial year runs from 1 July to 30 June. So as of 30 June, the actual profit for this company is $100,000. The tax payable will be $30,000. If the company lodges its own tax return, it will be due by 31 October in that year. However, if the company engages a tax agent to lodge the income tax return, it may not be due for lodgement until March of the following calendar year—that is, nine months after the end of the financial year. This on the face of it seems fantastic because businesses get to retain those funds for longer, which is true. However, if this money has not been set aside or budgeted for, then I find that most businesses have spent the money on growing the business further and don't have the funds available to pay the ATO when it is due. Can you see the big issue arising here?

Another issue is the PAYG Instalment system. The company can lodge its tax return anytime from July until March of the following year. Generally, most businesses don't lodge their first tax return until as late as possible. Once the return is lodged, the ATO then makes an assumption that the profit earned in the previous financial year will be earned again in the current financial year and will issue a PAYG Instalment notice requesting the company to pay approximately the full amount of tax as the previous year, in this example, $30,000. (Note the ATO will apply a CPI increase to the previous year.) Normally, the obligation of the company is to pay this quarterly; however, because this is the catch up of the first three-quarters of the financial year, the ATO can levy a full year in June. This results in a further $30,000 of tax being due and payable in July. For the business owner, this means that you will need to pay two years' tax in the space of four months. Ouch. Can you see how important that budgeting is now?

When you lodge your tax return for the second year, this tax paid is a credit against the tax payable on the profit. So if your second year of trading had the same profit as your first ($100,000), then there will be no further tax to pay. However, if the business has increased the profit for the year, for example, to $150,000, then there will be tax payable of $15,000 when the company lodges its income tax return ($45,000 tax less $30,000 PAYG Instalment) to allow for the increased income. This can be the make or break in the cash flow for the business.

There is an ability to vary the amount of tax levied on your BAS if you estimate your profit will be less in the current financial year as compared to the previous year. However, if the profit is more, there is an obligation to pay an increased amount. (Note: It is not a recommended strategy to decrease your estimated profit, as you will need to make payment one way or the other. Again, seek that professional specialist advice before you take action.)

Then on your September BAS, you will be obligated to pay approximately $7,500 per quarter for that current year's tax, that is, the third year of trading.

All of these tax payments should be included in your cash flow forecast. Some accountants will budget for them in the profit and loss, but most will include them in the cash flow forecast as part of the balance sheet liabilities. I am not fussed whether you include them in your budget profit and loss and then your cash flow forecast or just your cash flow forecast, as long as you do it.

One of the biggest criticisms I hear from business owners wishing to change accountants is their current accountant advising them of a large tax bill that's payable the next day. There was no warning. Everyone hates surprise bills, even small ones, but tax is usually a large bill, which makes it worse. To reduce any risk of surprises, for our Virtual CFO customers we typically project two years' of tax liabilities for our business owners, so there are no surprises. We update this forecast every month based on the projected profit of the business. While we may not be 100% correct, we are at least keeping the business owners aware of their obligations so they don't spend the cash before considering their future tax obligations.

Working Capital

What is working capital? Working capital is the funding (cash flow or loan) your business requires to operate on a day-to-day basis. If you do not have sufficient funds available to pay for your suppliers, creditors and wages, you will go out of business. You require available funds to meet your short-term liabilities.

To commence your business, you need capital (cash flow or loan) to set the business up. Then you need working capital to ensure the business continues. So what are you actually funding? When you open your doors to start operating your business, you need to pay for expenses, which are incurred before cash from sales starts rolling in. In a business that sells services, the main costs will be in the form of wages for you and your staff. (I just heard some of you laugh at this because I know that some of you have not or did not pay yourself a wage in the early days of your business.) In a business that sells goods, you will have to purchase the stock before you sell it.

If you sell services that take multiple days to deliver, then it is important to measure the days it takes from commencing providing service until the invoice is raised. This is known as work in progress (WIP). This measures the efficiency of delivery of the service. The longer the days, potentially the less efficient the business is and the larger the working capital funding is required. WIP can be a big problem for businesses that sell professional services like accountants, lawyers and IT consultants. This was an issue for my accounting firm for a number of years. Our WIP days were too high for a long period of time. The main reason was due to the number of jobs our team worked on at any given time. They were working on too many jobs at one time, which led to a lack of focus in finishing the jobs. To resolve this we reduced the number of jobs on hand and provided a structure to focus on completion. This reduced the number of WIP days in the practice by half, from 40 to 20 days. This is now in line with our service commitment that all year-end compliance services provided to our customers will be completed within three weeks of having all the information to commence. There are also many other strategies that can be implemented, like invoicing the job in stages. The strategies become fairly evident once you understand the issue and focus on a solution.

If you sell goods, you need to ascertain the number of days it takes from ordering and paying for the goods to selling them. Once again, the shorter the period of time it takes from payment of the goods until the invoicing of your customer, the lower the working capital requirements.

However, the mere invoicing of the goods or services does not immediately reduce the need for working capital funding if you provide terms to your customers. As indicated in the previous chapter, customers may not pay you within the terms that you offer, 7, 14, 21 or 30 days. If it takes, on average, 45 days to be paid after you invoice your customers, you need to add this to the number of days it takes from the purchase of goods or the commencement of the services until the invoice date. Let's look at some numbers. If it takes 40 days from the commencement of the job until the completion and invoice, then an additional 45 days to get paid, that means it takes 85 days (in total) to get paid from the commencement of the work. This means you need sufficient working capital to fund the expenses that will be incurred in the 85 days for the business to survive. This can be crippling for a small business.

The best way to predict the working capital is to complete the budget profit and loss and the cash flow forecast. The balance of a cash flow forecast indicates the projected cash in the bank at the end of each month. The deficiency in cash funds available at the end of the month will indicate the working capital required. When you project the monthly cash balance for the following twelve months, the biggest cash deficiency is the minimum working capital required to operate the business. So the more strategies that you can implement to reduce your working capital requirements, the less funding is required for your business.

Let me share a problem that we had in our business. You may wonder, 'How can an accountant and business advisor have a problem in his business? Shouldn't he know it all?' The answer is yes, we know most things about running an efficient and profitable business; however, that doesn't necessarily mean that we always take our own advice or 'medicine' as I call it. It is like the plumber with the leaky tap or the mechanic with the broken-down car. Sometimes we don't look after ourselves as well as we look after our customers. Getting back to us, we had a fairly large debtor issue. On average, it was taking 113 days to be paid by our customers. That is over three months. I know you're thinking, 'That is disgraceful. How did you let this happen?' Well, here is my take on the performance. If you have customers that are having financial difficulty and you are assisting them to correct their issues, I found it hard to then ask them to pay their accounting fees. The issue was that we were too nice. As much as I love my customers, I love my family more, so the motivation to ensure that we got paid as early as possible was to ensure that my family did not suffer as a consequence.

The key with reducing debtors is prevention, not cure. Most businesses will naturally focus on the problem of debtors once the debtor has been created (the customer has not paid the invoice raised). They will do this by putting in place a debt collection strategy. Whilst this is important if you have an existing problem, it is a better outcome if you can eliminate the debtor from existing in the first place. One strategy is to offer a discount if payment is received up front before the work for that customer commences. Make sure that the discount is sufficient for the customer to be motivated enough to take it, but not so much that it cuts too much into your profit margin so you are losing money. Another strategy is to sign your customers up for direct debit transfers. With these strategies, we reduced our average debtor days from 113 to 40 days. Based on our turnover, that meant we had $400,000 extra in our bank account, which meant we no longer needed to rely on our overdraft. Further, we saved more money, as we were no longer paying interest to the bank. The great part of these strategies was that it did not compromise our relationship with our customers. We still have a debt collection policy and procedure, but we use it less and less often. Our goal is to have negative WIP (that is, most work is paid up front) and zero debtors. This goal is achievable if you have policies and stick to them. The point is to be very up front with your customers, advise them of your terms and ensure they are educated when they go outside of them.

There is more power in saying 'No' than 'Yes'; especially when it comes to being selective about the types of customers you will be providing goods and services to.

Hopefully, I have convinced you of the importance of preparing a budget and a cash flow forecast, and now you have the tools and knowledge to implement them. May you never have a cash flow problem ever again.

SUCCESS TIP
There is only one success tip for this chapter: make sure that you complete a cash flow forecast before you commence trading, and ensure that it is updated every month.

Chapter 7

WHO'S DRIVING?

Leadership

Obviously, to have a business you need at least one person commencing it, in this case, you, the business owner. Because you are one person, you can only achieve so much; if you want to grow your business beyond yourself, you must employ resources. Resources can come in the form of equipment like computers or machinery or intellectual property (written material). Or they come in the form of humans. Human resources, as the name suggests, are the people that work in your business to help grow it beyond you. Pretty obvious, eh, but I just thought I'd put it into perspective for the readers who have not thought of it like this before. Sometimes it's the little observations that make the biggest difference.

In previous chapters I've discussed how to measure your business's value, which was a combination of profit multiplied by the risk of achieving the profit in the future. (Business Value = Future Maintainable Earnings × Capitalisation Rate.) When you commence employing people, you generally are increasing both at the same time. Why? People provide you with leverage to complete tasks that you do not have the time and resources yourself to complete. People increase your capacity, which increases profit. Employing people also decreases the amount of business that rests on your shoulders, thus decreasing the risk in the business. If we think about the valuation methodology, and there is only one person in the business and that is you, the likelihood of the business continuing to achieve the profits it has historically achieved will be significantly reduced if you no longer work in the business. This will result in a low capitalisation rate, thus resulting in a low business value.

By employing people, you are reducing the risk that comes from the business relying solely upon you as the owner, resulting in a higher capitalisation rate and therefore increased business value.

Business profits do not grow in a straight upward line; they tend to grow in a jagged upwards motion. What I mean by this is that before you employ your first person, you will be more profitable immediately before you employ the person, then less profitable immediately after, because you will have incurred costs before you can generate income from the increased resource costs in your business. This not always the rule, but it's true in 90% of cases.

Employing people can be one of the most satisfying experiences you can have as a business owner, but it can also be one of the biggest headaches. It is not just the stress of ensuring there is sufficient cash flow to pay your employees; there's also the emotional stress that comes with people who you are ultimately responsible for in your business.

There are a few things that you can do to ensure that the experience of employing people is a very positive and satisfying one. These tips will also assist you in achieving your business goals and aspirations. The first one that I will share with you is to build the infrastructure before you employ. I know that this is difficult, because in the early stages of your business, you are time-poor and the reason you are employing people is to free up your time. Even if you are recruiting a person to help you build your infrastructure, you should at least do the following before you hire:

- Document your Vision and Values
- Prepare a standard code of conduct and letter of offer that complies with statutory obligations
- Document and present the job outline and KPIs of the position
- Establish a formal review process outlining how the reviews will be conducted and the timing of those reviews

These are the minimum requirements that an employer needs to have in place before employing anyone to ensure they are a responsible employer. Some of it follows on from Chapter 1 to ensure that you have great clarity on your Vision, Why and Values.

SUCCESS TIP
Do not employ anyone until you have the legal documentation and a review process in place.

Being clear on what you expect in the role and from the person is extremely important. One of the main reasons why people fail early on in a role is due to poor communication between the person responsible for the new employee and the employee. I find that communication problems rest largely with the employer. We will spend the rest of this chapter discussing how you can be an employer of choice, where people bang down the door to want to work for your business.

The main distinction between success and failure in business is strong leadership. Business owners who are strong leaders will more likely have successful businesses than business owners who don't have these skills. Leadership is the key to business success. I've seen this in the results that the business owners obtain once they go through a leadership program that I have taught, specifically designed for small business owners to help become better leaders.

In the course, I teach business owners what it takes to become better leaders. The course is based on John C. Maxwell's book, *The 21 Irrefutable Laws of Leadership*. If you are looking to read a book to assist you in becoming a better leader, I can highly recommend this one. Maxwell is an expert on leadership and does consulting for Fortune 500 companies. The only issue is that his teachings are very U.S.-centric, so I spent considerable time converting his teachings to Australian conditions.

As with anything, there is nothing new in the world of business teachings; it is more how they are packaged and presented. Let me summarise what I believe are the most important traits of a leader.

Why is leadership so important? Your business is a reflection of its business owner. The following is an excerpt from the teachings of Maxwell:

Personnel	determines the potential
Relationships	determines the morale
Structure	determines the size
Vision	determines the direction
Leadership	determines the success of the organisation

Understanding each of these statements is required for the business to be successful; however, without strong leadership, the others will not be achieved to the fullest extent. Leadership is the foundation of a successful business.

So what is leadership? Leadership can be measured by the level of influence that you have over people. It is not based on position or title; it is voluntary. Following a leader is a voluntary act. You follow a leader because you want to, not because you have to. So if you want to have a business where people are banging down the door to get in, you need to have strong leadership qualities. Many people get confused between the traits of a manager and the traits of a leader. A manager will require you to do things right, whereas a leader influences you to do the right thing. Managers are very task-oriented, whereas leaders are more inspirational and motivational.

When I am speaking to business owners about their leadership skills, I ask them to rate out of ten their leadership capabilities, one being poor and ten being the best leader that could not be improved upon. Whilst this measure is very subjective because it is based on self-assessment, it is usually a fairly accurate reflection of their abilities (unless of course the business owner is delusional). Most business owners will rate themselves between three and eight. The important point to note about this is that none of us are tens. The beginning of a great leader is knowing they can improve on their leadership capabilities.

What makes a good leader? There is an argument that great leaders are born, meaning it is part of their DNA. Whilst I agree that some people are born with leadership skills and instincts, I do not believe that this means they will be the best leaders. Some of us are lucky enough to be born with such skills, but what about the rest? Based on my experience, it seems that whether you were blessed with leadership skills or not, you can always improve. The natural born leaders still need to learn and develop their skills just like people that were not blessed with the same. I also do not believe that it's that black and white that you either have leadership skills or you don't. Like any human traits, there are degrees of abilities. So even if your leadership skills are not natural, you can improve them and become a leader.

You may already find that you are a leader of sorts. Leadership comes in many different shapes and sizes. You may be a father or mother and therefore leading your children to live a full life. You may be a coach of a child's sporting team, which shapes the lives of many. You may be a volunteer supporting and guiding the people around you. Leadership is not just confined to business. Remember, leadership is about influence. Think about whom you influence and what skills you are demonstrating and putting into practice from a leadership perspective. Ask yourself, what are your strengths with regards to your leadership capabilities, and what challenges do you have and how do you think that you can overcome them? Do you need to overcome them? Can you use resources to fill the gap with your challenges?

> **SUCCESS TIP**
> Become self-aware of your leadership ability. Then fine-tune your strengths and overcome your challenges.

So how do you improve your leadership skills and abilities? There are some really easy, practical tips that I am going to share with you now to start you on the right path. Remember, if you get the leadership piece right, then everything—especially team alliance—falls into place.

One of the most important lessons that I teach that really resonates with business owners is about the most important leadership traits. To highlight this, I show business owners the following table.

The true measure of leadership is *influence.*

Rank	Characteristic	Percentage
1	Leading by example	26%
2	Strong ethics and morals	19%
3	Knowledge of the business	17%

Rank	Characteristic	Percentage
4	Fairness	14%
5	Overall intelligence and competence	13%
6	Recognition of employees	10%

This table reflects the results of a study completed by Ajilon Finance, a U.S.-based company that polled its employees. It highlights that leading by example is considered the most important trait of a leader. This supports the idea that most people learn visually. Think about this on a deeper level. From the day we were born, we started learning by observing, because we could not process words at that stage. We are effectively wired to observe to learn, which drives our behaviour. Whilst effective communication is required to get the message across, people are very aware—even more so nowadays—that words are just words unless they are backed up by actions.

But what example are you supposed to portray? The best answer to this is to consider an influencer that you look up to. This person may be known personally to you, or may not, such as famous icons. Regardless, you have observed them and like what you see, otherwise you would not be influenced by them. Oh, as a side note, influencers can be good and bad; there are plenty of examples of leaders who were leading for the wrong reasons and had catastrophic consequences for the world, like horribly devastating wars. Working on the principle that we understand right from wrong, based on a socially acceptable culture, consider the people that influence you. The idea is to then mimic the way they present themselves and how they conduct themselves. If you have this in the forefront of your mind, you are more likely to start influencing the people around you.

There are a number of people that I admire, who help focus me on the type of person that I would like to be as a leader. There are people who are not famous, and others who are. People in my leadership training course are often surprised to hear that one of the leaders I admire most is Steve Irwin, the Crocodile Hunter. What I respected most about

Steve was his contagious passion. The first time I ever saw Steve was on one of his crocodile hunter shows, I thought that he was as mad as a cut snake. Then I was intrigued as to what drove him. I couldn't help but notice his passion for the environment and the animal world.

Then I visited the Australia Zoo. It was once his father's before Steve took it on and developed it into a national tourist attraction. I was absolutely fascinated by the place. It was the cleanest, friendliest place I have ever been to. You could see how engaged all the staff were with the place, and you knew that it was driven by Steve's passion and leadership. Upon his death, I read the book Steve's wife, Terri wrote, titled *My Steve*. It provided a wonderful insight into the man and gave me a deeper understanding of the type of person and leader Steve was. I encourage you to read this book. Steve was a man who was an extremely strong, uncompromising leader, but also a man who was genuine and simple in his approach to life. The closest I came to meeting Steve was getting my photo taken with a life-sized cardboard cutout. It was a tragedy that he died so young. It reminds me to keep on track and keep focused to achieve what I can, while I can.

The other person I admire as a leader is Rudolph Giuliani. Giuliani was the mayor of New York City when the September 2011 terrorist attack occurred. The days that followed must have been unbelievable. I read his book *Leadership* and found it extremely interesting. It's a valuable read. The most important trait that I think that Giuliani had was the ability to calm a city that was in complete chaos. He did this through a combination of strength, focus, discipline and empathy. In the days following, he had a morning meeting to focus all of the different service departments to co-ordinate the day's activities. He personally attended six funerals a day and all funerals were attended by at least one of his staff. There are so many great examples of leadership in this book, and that's why I'm recommending it to you.

Think about the people you admire as a leader. From the first moment that you open the front door of your business until you close it up for the day, ask yourself the following questions:

- Do I look like a leader?

- Do I act like a leader?

- Do I talk like a leader?

- Do I walk like a leader?

I am in the fortunate position of being able to go into businesses and observe their cultures. When I am sitting in reception before I meet with the owners, I make it a point to observe everything. It is amazing how much you learn about a business sitting in reception. After about five minutes, I am able to pick up what is going on in the business from a cultural perspective watching people's interactions. You have heard the saying 'fish stink from the head'? Well, never a truer statement was made with respect to a business. The business owner is responsible for setting the culture of the business.

Because I am highly competitive, I turn this into a game that I play by myself. How well did I spot the issues of the business and the deficiencies/weaknesses/challenges of the owner whilst sitting in reception? Without sounding conceited, I can usually pick up most things. When I ask business owners what their biggest challenge is and if they respond with 'employees', generally I have already worked this out based on the behaviour of what I have seen from the reception area. We will talk about employees more in Chapter 8.

Maybe this is you or someone you know. When I sit in a reception area, and I see people enter the office in the morning, some people—especially business owners—walk right into the business, straight past all of their employees, head into their office and start working. They don't say hello. They don't provide any eye contact. They simply walk straight past. This astounds me. This behaviour is louder than any other noise and says so much, and certainly at the basic level it is bad manners. I don't undertand how you can see people that work with you and then ignore them. From a leadership perspective, this is one of the ultimate examples of poor leadership and behaviour. You're leading by example and demonstrating that it's okay to act like this in the business. This is not conducive to building a cohesive team. If you or someone in your organisation does this, stop it. There is no simpler way to say it. You don't treat anyone else in your life like this. Why would you treat your team this way?

People look to leaders to understand how to act. One day I decided that I was tired of wearing ties with my suit to work every day. I found that they were contributing to more neck injuries; so I thought that at the age of forty, I could stop wearing one. Now before I do anything, I always consider the ramifications of my actions. I knew that my customers and prospective customers wouldn't mind; however, I wondered what my team would do. We had a dress code which stipulated corporate attire, but it did not specifically mention if a tie was required. Anyway, sure enough over the next month, I observed that one by one the males in the office stopped wearing ties. They didn't converse with me or anyone else on the team as to know whether it was appropriate; they just started to do so of their own accord. Eventually, I told them that I was observing their behaviour about not wearing a tie; everyone had a good laugh when I told them what had happened. Some were acutely aware of what had happened, whilst others made their own decision based on what I did. If you think that your staff are not watching you, then think again.

SUCCESS TIP
Demonstrate the behaviour that you wish your team to demonstrate.

Another skill to possess in being a great leader is self-awareness. Being self-aware makes you a better leader. I once knew a business owner that had very poor self-awareness which caused a huge number of problems. His view of the world was very different from the world viewed by the people around him. This created poor communication and alignment in the team. It also resulted in high turnover of staff, multiple business partners leaving the business and numerous divorces. Not great statistics, but still he did not see that the problem was with him. It was quite fascinating to watch. One of the things that I found interesting was when he knew he was lying about something and as the lie came out of his mouth, it would become fact to him. It was like a lie filter. So it came out as a lie and then entered his ears as fact; because he heard it, albeit from himself, he believed it to be true. When I have spoken to many business owners since, they all know someone like that, so it must be a common condition. The other problem was that he had a tremendous ego, which is also not conducive to becoming an effective leader and building a high-performing team. This ego never allowed him to self-assess and consider that maybe the reason people were leaving was because of him. There was an element of delusion in his behaviour that was evidently clear for those inside and outside of the business.

SUCCESS TIP
Being self-aware is extremely important for you to be an effective leader.

If you are concerned that you may possess these traits, complete this exercise. Ask three of the people you trust and respect to write a list of your strengths, weaknesses and challenges. Write your own independent list and then compare the lists and identify the gaps. This exercise will highlight how self-aware you are. Make sure that you select people that you know will be honest; avoid those who will feel pressured into telling you what you want to hear.

Chapter 8

HAVE WE GOT THE RIGHT PEOPLE IN THE RIGHT SEATS?

Organisational Structure and Team Alignment

Leadership is important and is the foundation piece of great team alignment and performance. Remember, your business is a reflection of you, so if there is a problem, like a poor performing team or high staff turnover, it is usually because of . . . that's right, YOU. You hire, you train, you support, you guide, you you you. If I had a $1 for every time I heard someone whingeing about another generation, I could have retired a long time ago. My take on this is that every generation has certain traits; however, not everyone in the generation is the same. There is good and bad behaviour. The aim is to find the people who will fit with your business. I guarantee that they are out there, and I've proven this with my business. My business is mostly made up of people born from the 1980's onward, and I have to say that I have the most efficient, dedicated, hard-working team, and I am hugely proud of them. But it was not always this way. I previously experienced high turnover and poor performance, just like most of my customers. I also spent between $80,000-$100,000 per annum on recruitment fees, which was a disproportionate amount compared to our turnover at the time. I was extremely frustrated and unhappy with the performance of the firm. Having said that, we were performing very well as compared to our competitors. It's just that I do not accept mediocrity.

What I am about to suggest may offend some. Some of what I am about to say is a generalisation, to prove a point. So if I offend, I apologise in advance. (Reading *Outliers* by Malcolm Gladwell or *Drive* by Daniel Pink may assist in better understanding my reasoning.)

So what did I do? I changed my recruitment policy for one. I no longer looked to the elite universities or schools as a background for the candidate to recruit from. I no longer employed people in the two-to-five year bracket of employment experience. (In our industry these were the hardest people to find, and the ones available were generally not in line with any business values.) About ten years ago, I started a graduate recruitment program for the purposes of home-growing our talent. This took a lot of effort because you have to build the infrastructure to support and develop young professionals. But I can say the results have been outstanding. Once we built the model, we then started recruiting.

Our goal has been to recruit one new graduate every six months. (I realise that in comparison to a large business this may not be many.) The reason for one every six months was to ensure that they got the nurturing, care and support they needed from myself and my trusted senior team members.

Whom did we recruit? I profiled myself and the people I knew who were successful in our business, in order to understand the backgrounds and traits that seemed to work. We then started to form a profile of the people that we were looking for. This is when we started to generalise. What we were looking for were accounting graduates, who graduated from practical tertiary institutions—and not the ones that commanded the best marks to get in. These graduates have come from the country or via mid-tier private schools or high schools with traditional working class backgrounds. Why these people? We were looking for young people that had strong work ethics and had to work to get to where they got to. They were the hungry ones that seemed to have fewer of the generational traits that many people seemed to whinge about. My philosophy is that I can teach the technical; I can't change attitudes, because that is wired from parents, peers and background. Now, I know that you can turn people around if you give them a chance—no matter what background they come from. But as a business owner, you need to be commercial. I want a person whom I know is in line with our values rather than a person who will resist instruction. I still have people that don't work out; however, the ratio is significantly reduced from what it was.

In the last ten years, the team has built itself, and the culture is awesome. The best part is that I can't take the credit for it because the team has taken the opportunity and run with it. As many of you know, it is not as simple as getting the recruitment right. There must be a constant and consistent effort to ensure that your team is performing at an elite level.

Once your team is on board, how do you ensure that they are retained, developed, aligned and becoming a high-functioning team? This is where emotional intelligence comes in, also known as EQ or EI.

For those not familiar with Emotional Intelligence, a very brief outline from Wikipedia is:

'Emotional intelligence (EI or EQ) is the capability of individuals to recognize their own, and other people's emotions, to discern between different feelings and label them appropriately, to use emotional information to guide thinking and behaviour, and to manage and/or adjust emotions to adapt environments or achieve one's goal(s).

Although the term first appeared in a 1964 paper by Michael Beldoch, it gained popularity in the 1995 book by that title, written by the author, psychologist, and science journalist Daniel Goleman. Since this time, Goleman's 1995 analysis of EI has been criticized within the scientific community, despite prolific reports of its usefulness in the popular press.'

Take it or leave it, as you deem appropriate to your circumstances.

People complete IQ (Intelligence Quotient) tests to determine how intelligent they are. However, having a high IQ does not mean that the person will have a high EQ. In many cases, it usually is the opposite: people with high IQs can have very poor EQs. EQ is all about being in tune with your emotions at all times, especially in stressful situations, and being able to perceive, respect and influence the emotions of others. If you have a low EQ, there are things that you can do to increase your EQ. The more EQ you have, the better chance you have in building the ultimate team and business. There are lots of ways to increase your EQ, but for the rest of the chapter I am going to concentrate on the three tools that I know will have the biggest impact on your EQ and therefore your leadership capabilities.

The more that you can understand people, the better you can support and nurture them to achieve their full potential. How can you understand and support people better? Let's look more closely at the three tools that I usually use.

The first tool is to understand people's communication preferences. One of the best ways to understand more of the science around communication is to study Neuro-Linguistic Programming (NLP). The founders of NLP are Richard Bandler and John Grinder. NLP provides an explanation as to how individuals communicate. There are four distinct types of communication: visual, auditory, kinesthetic and digital (VAKD). Most people will have two of these as their preferred preference of communication. Before I explain these communication preferences, I want to highlight the importance of understanding these different styles. If you understand how people prefer to communicate, you are better able to influence them in the direction of the business. It is a significant tool to understand, and everyone that I have introduced to this science enjoys significantly improved communication with the people around them, which is a benefit to everyone.

One of the best ways I find to explain the concept of VAKD is by way of example.

This example also highlights the different ways people make buying decisions. Think about when you walk into a car sales showroom or car yard to purchase a car. Think about what is important to you when you are looking to buy a car. Then compare yourself to the following four individuals to see which one or ones are most closely aligned with your communication and buying preferences.

Person Number One comes into the showroom; her name is Victoria. When she walks into the showroom, she spots a car that takes her fancy. A sales assistant approaches her and asks if she can help her.

Victoria tells the sales assistant that she really likes the look of that car over there. She loves the colour and its styling and could really see herself driving that car. Victoria is showing signs that she is a high visual communicator based on the language she is using. She uses words like 'see' and 'look' which drive and motivate her. This also indicates that if you want to communicate effectively with Victoria, you need to show her pictures and visual aids. Whilst these people will also have a preference for other communication styles, they will need to see things or be shown to ensure that the message is received.

Next, Person Number Two, let's name her Adelaide, comes into the showroom. When Adelaide walks in, she heads over to a car and gets in. A sales assistant approaches her and asks if he can help her. Adelaide is playing with the sound system. She then asks the sales assistant if he has the keys to start the engine. Once the car starts, she listens to the engine and revs the motor to accentuate the sound. Adelaide says to the sales assistant, 'Listen to the engine! It sounds finely tuned—and that stereo system is great. The subwoofers really provide a deep base to the music. I love it!' This person has high auditory communication preferences. These people prefer you to use words and sounds to get your message across. You have to be very careful how you speak to an auditory person, as they listen to every word. They are usually moved by music and their moods are influenced by the sounds that they hear. You can tell an auditory communicator even in their written language, as they are usually the ones that write things on emails like, 'That sounds great.' They usually correct you on your language and assist you with finding the right words whilst you are speaking to them.

Person Number Three comes into the showroom; his name is Kevin. When he walks into the showroom, he gets straight into a car. A sales assistant approaches him and asks if he can help. The sales assistant finds Kevin in the car moving his hand over the leather seats and getting comfortable. He also finds him touching the steering wheel. Kevin says to the sales assistant that he loves the feel of the leather seats and the woodgrain steering wheel. He thinks the driving position of this car feels really comfortable. Kevin has a high preference for touch and therefore is kinesthetic. Kinesthetic people are tactile and they have a preference to communicate via experiencing the touch and feel of things. While giving presentations, a kinesthetic learner might like to hold things in his hands like a pen or a pointer. He'll find that holding something provides himself with a grounding. Speaking from experience, for some reason I learn and present much better when I have a whiteboard marker or a pointer in my hand. I can't explain it, but it just makes me find the right words to use.

Daniel, Person Number Four, the final person comes into the show-room. When he walks into the showroom, he goes over to a car and lifts the bonnet. The sales assistant approaches him and asks if he can help. Daniel starts to ask the sales assistant questions about the specifications of the car, like how much kilowatt output the car provides, what the fuel efficiency is and towing capacity. Daniel wants to know that the car is a good value for the money, in comparison to other cars in its class. So Daniel is after the details associated with the car because he is a highly digital person. A digital person wants to know all the facts and figures. Interestingly enough, often the digital person lifts the bonnet but does not even know what he is looking at—he is just compelled to look. There are a number of professions that a digital person is more suited to, such as engineering, air traffic control, and accountancy. They communicate and learn through detail.

How does knowing this information help businesses perform better? Understanding people's communication preferences helps you to be more efficient and effective with your communication and therefore you can get the best out of people. It will lower staff turnover and re-duce frustration in an organisation by reducing conflict. If you know a person's communication preference, then you will most likely know the best approach to get your message across. For example, if you are naturally a big picture person and you are approaching a detail-oriented person, then you need to change your natural style of communicating to be more aligned to a detailed style. If you approach a detail person in your natural style of big picture, they will struggle to follow you, because they are constantly seeking to understand if what you say will work. One of the best ways to communicate with detail people is to start with the big picture and then talk through the step-by-step process to achieve the goal.

> **SUCCESS TIP**
> Better understand your own and your team's communication preference/s. Commence a profile of each team member.

The second tool I utilise is personality profiling.

At some stage in most people's lives, they have been exposed to personality profiling. You may have heard of Myers-Briggs or McQuaig or DISC. These are personality profiling tools that assess what type of person you are. Personality profiling can assist to better understand ourselves and the people around us. It is used predominantly in businesses intially in recruiting to determine who is the most suitable candidate to get the job and then in business to help teams be more sensitive to the different personality types that make up the organisation.

The profiling tool is a series of questions that you answer, generally asking you your thoughts on different situations. Some of them also get you to rank different words to different questions to get an insight into how you think. Once the questions have been answered, a report is completed. The reports provide a wonderful insight into how you think about things and what preferences you have in relation to the type of work you enjoy or are naturally better at.

Every time I have completed these profiles, I realised things about myself that I was not conscious of. In one of my profiles, it indicated that I avoid detail. This was really difficult for me to comprehend because I am an accountant by trade, and my life is detail. However, it went on to say that I prefer to think big picture rather than about all the little details. I started to think about this further. I then realised that with this preference, I am more motivated when I can create concepts and look forward to what is possible. This insight aligns with the entrepreneurial skills that I possess. The final comment which made me more comfortable was that whilst I avoid detail, if I am forced to complete detailed tasks, I do them better than most. When I reflected on how I operate, I realised it was true. It explained why I have evolved beyond being an accountant to being a business advisor, an entrepreneur who has created an acccounting firm that is a complete business advisory firm focused on inspiring business owners in their journey to achieve the dream as to why they went into business in the first place.

This information was hugely powerful for me because it allowed me to understand how I operate. A big picture person is generally the opposite to a detail-oriented person. This means that I was in conflict with myself when I was working in my business. Now that I understand that, naturally I would prefer to stay in the big picture mindset, but I know that I am also good at working with the detail. I have comfort in both these traits. Now I am more conscious of giving myself permission to work the details when required, rather than fighting it. As a business owner of an accounting firm, this duality is actually a blessing because it allows me to create, grow and develop the business whilst ensuring that I am doing it in a measured and methodical way.

One of the best profiling tools that I have found is DISC. The word DISC is an acronym: Dominance, Influence, Steadiness, Conscientiousness. These words explain the four different types of personalities. Like NLP, you will have a personality preference for two out of the four.

(Note that DISC looks at types and styles of personalities; here I have only listed types for simplicity. If you find these of interest, you can read further about the program on the DISC website.)

Let's look at each one of these personality types (as per the DISC website https://www.discprofile.com/what-is-disc/overview/):

Dominant: Person places emphasis on accomplishing results, the bottom line—confidence.

Influence: Person places emphasis on influencing or persuading others, openness, relationships.

Steadiness: Person places emphasis on cooperation, sincerity, dependability.

Conscientiousness: Person places emphasis on quality and accuracy, expertise, competency.

The real power in personality profiling comes from the knowledge you get from the report, both from self-awareness and from better understanding the people around you. I use profiling to help align teams. Generally, teams are not aligned when there is a poor understanding of the people they work with or with communication between team members. By teaching the different types of personalities that exist, people can become more sensitive and empathic towards the people around them. The real benefit is that the team members become more patient and tolerant around each other. It is facinating to see the acknowledgement of differences and how that transforms interactions and relationships. Sometimes at the end of the sessions, it is like there is a feeling of a big group hug. I love seeing the connections that start to form.

To assist with helping people to become more aware of the different personality types as seen above, in our sessions we'll assign an animal to each type for easier understanding. To ensure that the teaching remains a focus and is not lost after the lesson fades, the animals are placed on the desks or workstations of the employee which best represents their personality type.

By the way, some people have no preference for a type—they adapt to each type depending on the situation. When I was profiled, I was one of these people. However, when you delve deeper, there is usually a preference. These people are often referred to as 'balanced', as they fit in the middle of the quadrant. My actual preference is Influence. I know this because this is where I am happiest and most comfortable. This is known as your heart space. While my second preference is Conscientiousness (sometimes referred to as Compliance), this is largely because I live in a compliant world surrounded by compliant people (accountants). This is largely driving the second preference at present. It will be interesting to see if this preference changes if I no longer operate an accounting firm. (Not that I have any plans to change—because I love what I do and can't imagine doing anything else. I love my business, my career and my work. It is hugely rewarding, challenging and diverse. What I love the most is that I have the opportunity to influence people to change their lives for the better, and that is pretty humbling.)

> **SUCCESS TIP**
> Ensure that you choose a personality profiling tool and use it in your business to recruit, manage and align your team.

The third tool that I use to assist people to increase their EQ is the five love languages. In presentations when I mention that we are going to discuss love languages, I am usually met with the bemusement of the audience or participants. Perhaps people think, 'What is an accountant/ business advisor doing talking about love?' They think that business must be professional and corporate. But a lot of powerful lessons that lead to great success are actually psychological and emotional.

I was given a book by a mentor during a conversation that I was having with her about the fact that I did not feel like I was connecting with one of my sons. The book is called *The Five Love Languages* by Dr. Gary Chapman. In summary, the five love languages are:

1. Words of Affirmation (telling someone what you appreciate about them)
2. Quality of Time (spending focused, purposeful time with someone)
3. Gift Giving and Receiving (giving someone a present you know they'll enjoy)
4. Acts of Service (doing things for someone else)
5. Physical Touch (handshakes, high fives, etc.)

What do love languages have to do with business? The relationship be-tween the two is reward and appreciation. This is significantly important because of another statistic that I came across as to why employees leave organisations. Apparently the top reason why people either stay or leave organisations is about receiving appreciation for what they con-tribute. If you ask business owners, you may get a different response, and that different response is money. In these surveys conducted, money usually ranks between three and five. Appreciation and job satisfaction usually ranked as one or two. Therefore, it is important to show appreciation for your team members. Why don't we spend more time understanding what employees want? Let's take a closer look.

The five love languages provide different ways of appreciating the people around us. Dr. Chapman has written specific books applying the love languages to children and also relationships in general. If you think about it, the people that you work with have needs that are the same in a work environment as in other aspects of their lives. The application of these languages may change based on the receiver. How you apply them to your spouse will look different from how you use them with a co-worker. Now that I have framed this for you, let's consider the different types of appreciation that you can show others.

In business we often link reward with an increase in remuneration, for example, a pay raise or a bonus. This is classed as a gift in love language terms (Item 3 on the list). However, not all people respond the same way to gifts. They may appreciate them at the time, but it can be soon lost if that is not their love language. You may have personally experienced this with either giving a bonus or receiving a bonus. What was the response to this after a couple of weeks? Did it lose its initial motivating force, or appreciation, since initially receiving it, or was it a constant reminder of the benefit received?

We need to look beyond gifts as there are four other types of appreci-ation. The first item on the list above is Words of Affirmation. Consider how often you actually compliment your team or your peers for the great work that they did. Or encourage them, to assist them in doing better next time. No doubt you have experienced a lift when you receive compliments and encouragements when you've done a good job. The foundation is that these words must be genuine and specific.

I was taught by a child psychologist, that when you give praise to children, be very specific. For example, when your daughter or son comes home from kinder with a painting that you know means a lot to them. Unfortunately, you have absolutely no idea what the picture is, other than a lot of random colours on a page. The best thing that you can do is show appreciation for their hard work. Comment on each specific colour and how you like them and the shapes that they create. A lot of parents fall into the trap of just saying they love the painting, or worse—asking what it is. Your child will offer what the image is once you show your appreciation. What you are actually doing is making the words of affirmation specific and relevant to the situation. When you do this, your words are more likely to be received and resonate with the receiver.

In any relationship, words are important. The words 'I love you' are probably the most important. Perhaps you've heard people say after their loved ones passed away, they realised they didn't tell their beloved how much they loved them often enough. Often the response to these people is that their friend or family member knew how much they loved them based on their acts of service. This can be a sign that Words of Affirmation may be the love language of the person who is now expressing regret. When in doubt about someone's love language, tell them that you appreciate them anyway. It can't hurt but it can make a massive difference. (I just realised that I sound like a counseller. At times, my customers did confide in me about their personal life on their business journeys, and sometimes their personal relationships did arise. Whilst I never consult outside my area of expertise and always refer people to experts when there are real issues, most of the time they were happy that someone listened.)

The second love language on the list is Quality of Time. Some people crave time with the people they respect, love and look up to. Actually this was the lesson that I learnt about my son. We know that all children want our time as parents; however, my son especially needed my time as a reward, to show appreciation and connection. You have heard the statement 'You can't buy love'; well, this is definitely the case with people who crave time. In my position as director, some of the young employees look up to me and value our time together. I am not saying that I am special; however, there is a certain level of responsibility that comes with any management position, so make sure you don't abuse the privilege. As per the mantra, associated with Google (whether you agree or not), 'Don't be evil.'

Gift Giving and Receiving is the third love language on the list. I mentioned that in business we think that providing gifts, like bonuses, is one of the only ways to reward staff, and this 'gift' is usually linked to the business's performance. However, since you now know the other languages, you can become more creative and thoughtful in the way you reward and show appreciation.

Next on the list is Acts of Service. Doing acts of service for people can really show how much you appreciate what they do for you. This can be as simple as making a cup of tea for one of your team members. In actual fact, a simple act like this can make all the difference to people who have a preference towards Acts of Service as their love language. Perhaps buying flowers does not envoke the response that you were hoping for. How about unpacking the dishwasher or doing the washing and ironing instead. If your partner's love language is Acts of Service, this will show them that you appreciate them by doing an act of service for them. The same applies at work. If you are merely doing what you are expected to, this is not an act of service. But if you do something for someone, that is going over and above, then this can truly help you connect with these employees or peers. I know that when my team does things for me that geniunely shows a level of support above and beyond their job description, it gives me a tremendous lift and drives me to look after them more. I get an overwhelming sense of gratitude because I feel this massive level of support. This can be particularly supporting during stressful times in the business.

One of the greatest displays of support that I receive happens when I put on a presentation. My team always pulls together to support me. It gives me a huge lift and inspires me to do a better job. Words cannot explain the joy and happiness it gives me.

The last love language on the list is Physical Touch. This is one that I do not suggest for the workplace. This is unfortunate for people who have a preference for physical touch. For a more politically correct version of Physical touch for the workplace, you could consider options such as putting your hand on someone's shoulder, which shows reassurance and support, handshakes, fist bumps and high fives. During a presentation to a group of business owners, a medical doctor in the audience suggested that it was acceptable to touch someone between the shoulder and the elbow. I like this exception; however, be extremely careful to pick your mark and only do this with people who have a preference for physical touch, because if they do not have this preference, it can have the opposite affect on the person. If people don't like physical touch, then they may feel any contact with them as an invasion of personal space. How do you know if someone prefers physical touch? They might be the type of person who stands closer to you than others. Maybe they even get criticised for invading personal space. A big warning, though, unless you know 100% that this is a person's preference, don't touch them because the ramifications can be detrimental for all parties.

By now you might be wondering how you can figure out what love languages the people around you 'speak'. This is usually easy to predict because ordinarily the love language that they communicate in is the one that they predominantly use for others. If they have a preference for Gifts Giving and Receiving, then they are usually the ones that buy things for other people. If they have a preference for Acts of Service, then they are the ones that are always doing something for others, like teaching them, making them a cup of tea or unpacking the dishwasher. These people are the ones that constantly ask if they can do something to help.

Another way to bring this to the surface is to hold a session with your team and explain love languages and then ask them what their love language preference is. This session is a lot of fun because team members really get into understanding their own, and other people in their lives, love language. I also hold this session with my customers' team members. These sessions are always great fun, and the results are excellent. It really starts to connect people and makes them understand each other better.

Personally, I know that my love languages are Physical Touch and Acts of Service. However, I make a conscious effort to 'speak' all five languages with the people around me.

SUCCESS TIP
Observe your team and work out what their love languages are based on how they reward and show appreciation for other people. Write it down as part of the profiles that you are forming for your staff.

In my business, I make sure that I understand the love languages for each person on the team to ensure that I show them the individualised appreciation they deserve. There are also team rewards that I provide where I attempt to cover off the first four love languages. There are a series of events that I put on for the team, one of which is known as Fun Day. This is the biggest event on the calendar for the team—they love it. It's a day of thanks and appreciation, and we've held it annually so often it is now a business tradition. Here's what I do. First, I block out a top-secret date in my team's diary. Next, I come up with an idea that I know everyone will appreciate and enjoy that also has a bit of a wow factor. I like to contain the event to one day; otherwise, it cuts into people's personal time—and I make sure it is a surprise, as that adds to the experience. Some of the events that we have enjoyed are:

- Flying to Sydney to do the Harbour Bridge climb and lunch in the Rocks district.

- A trip to the Yarra Valley via helicopter to a winery and a wine tasting tour and lunch. This was one of my favourites because as a kid, I wanted to be a helicopter pilot.

- Flying to King Island in a DC3 plane for the day to sample the local produce and have lunch.

- Cirque du Soleil for an unbelievably facinating show.

- Flying to the Gold Coast to visit Dreamworld and White-Water World. Another favourite experience, because I got to be a child again for a day. I spent most of my time on the water slides enticing anyone stupid enough to run around with me all day.

- One year I did something completely different and changed the day totally. This was mainly because the team's partners were complaining that they did not get invited to these events. To accommodate this, I booked a resort in the Yarra Valley and invited all of the team and their partners to stay the night. During the day, we went on a wine tour, and then we held a dinner in a private dining room. As with most of these occasions, it ended with the people singing badly in the piano bar.

- Another trip to Sydney involved a luxury boat to cruise around the harbour, eventually dropping us off at Manly to have a relaxing lunch. Suffice it to say, the plane ride home was noisy, but hilarious.

- In a local event, we took limousines to the races where the team were wined and dined.

- A trip across Bass Straits to Hobart, where we then flew in helicopters to a winery for lunch. Next door was a whiskey distillery that had a testing tour. That plane ride home was another noisy one.

- Back to the Gold Coast where we spent the day at the Seaworld theme park. Another day of being a kid!

- Another local event was when the team rode horses on the beach on the Mornington Peninsula coastline, then relaxed in the hotsprings and ended up lunching at a nearby winery.

You can probably tell that I love putting on these events for my team. I have to say, though, that they are relatively stressful given that I have to ensure that I either equal or raise the bar each year, so there is no disappointment. Regardless, it's wonderful to see the team enjoy the day and talk about it later. We all get a buzz when the team can text their friends and family to tell them what they've been up to that day.

If you relate these event ideas back to the love languages, then they are covered in this one day. It is a gift to my team as a reward for effort; it is an act of service because it is something that I am doing for them that I organise. I am giving them time to enjoy and time with the directors and each other to experience. Usually during the day, I use words of thanks individually and to all for their commitment and effort to the business.

As a memento of the day, I take a photo with the team with an appropriate backdrop which I enlarge, frame and hang on the boardroom wall. This has multiple benefits. It serves as a reminder of the day so the appreciation lasts, and it also helps when recruiting new staff members, because it demonstrates my respect and gratitude for my team. It also inspires customers to see what they can do for their team to show appreciation.

The other events that we put on for our team revolve around physical activities. These events don't really have much to do with love languages, yet there are so many benefits that come from them. I am very much into health and fitness. One of my business partners is in his fifties, and he runs marathons around the world. He completed the New York City Marathon and also ran in Barcelona. We encourage our team to be fit and healthy, and lead by example. We have two regular events on our calendar, the BRW Corporate Running Relay and the Triathlon. The awesome part about these events is that we get a massive participation. In one of the first relay events we put on, we had eighteen out of twenty staff members participate. I don't think any other organisation could boast such statistics. The brilliant point to this is that through encouragement we are able to get a high level of participation. I love seeing people do things that they have never done before and see the sense of pride in their achievement. I joke that when they are employed in our business, we work on every aspect of them as a person. In reality, this is true.

Another reason I love the physical challenges we put on as events is that a lot of businesses merely focus on food and alcohol as part of their celebration events. We have that too, but I like to balance events up, because there's more to life than food and alcohol.

Chapter 9

WHERE TO NOW?

Business Growth Phases and Risk Management

When you start out in business, you're fuelled by hopes and dreams. Unfortunately for most, reality sets in pretty quickly after you commence business and generally it takes longer to get it off the ground than expected. The dollars don't flow into the business as fast as you would like or expect. When the bills start piling up, you may feel compelled to agree to any opportunity that comes your way. This wiring can continue to impact your business decisions, because as you get bigger and start to employ people, the need to gain as much business as possible only grows more urgent.

We are wired to think that if we say 'No' to business opportunities, they will run out. Unfortunately, by saying 'Yes' all of the time, we may not be making as much money as we possibly could (think back to the excavator business example in Chapter 5) or having an enjoyable business life. But there is a tremendous power in saying no. Whilst growth is exciting, it can also be dangerous for business, so risk mitigation strategies must be taken into consideration when making expansion decisions.

Businesses do not grow in a straight line. Every time you have the opportunity to grow, there are usually a whole lot of costs that go with the growth, which can make the business less profitable in the early stages of the expansion of the business.

So what are the different phases of business?

The different phases of business will depend on what type of business you're operating, for example, services, retail, wholesale, manufacturing, infrastructure, etc. This is because the immediate demands on the business internal infrastructure will differ for different businesses. The different types of business will also require different funding requirements. Some businesses will require employees immediately, whilst some businesses will only require the business owner to start and build before they must employ others.

The more requirements for working capital, the harder it can be to start; however, by starting this way you get a heads up and get over a significant hurdle immediately, which is, usually, employing your first staff member.

In simple terms, there are three distinct phases of every business: start-up, maturity and exit. There are many phases inside each of these three categories. Regardless of the phase, the discipline of business should not stop. From the day you start until the day you exit, you should be continuously building your business infrastructure and exercising discipline every day.

What infrastructure and discipline should you build into your business to ensure that the business is a great success? Let's take a look. I had a customer meeting with a business that was starting out. They operate a consulting business. There are four directors and shareholders, who are also the founders of the business. These guys are extremely smart operators in their field of expertise, kind of like rocket scientists. I have also been really impressed with their business concept, which is going to fix some significant world problems. However, it still amazes me that there are so many gaps. (This is not a criticism of these business owners; it's just that they only know what they know and cannot be an expert on all things.) For example, they were very clear about their business concept. But when I asked them how big they wanted to get, a $10m, $50m, or $100m value company, they were very unsure as to what that looked like. So I started to break this down for them. Because people are their main asset, I asked how many people they would like to work with in five years' time. They responded by saying that they thought it would be great to have thirty revenue-generating business development people with a team of talented people supporting them, so sixty employees in total. I asked how much revenue each business development person would support per annum. The CEO responded that they could support around $2m each. So it's possible that the total revenue of the company could be $60m. We then worked out that, based on the infrastructure build, the net profit on $60m would be around $20m. If we applied a capitalisation rate of three to five times, the business is potentially valued between $60m and $100m.

The CEO was so pleased that I was able to break it down, connect the dots and provide an outcome to the question. Now when he talks about what he wants to achieve, he has a clear picture to convey—one that gives him a direction and strategies to achieve that dream.

A fabulous tool that I use to help connect the dots is a One-Page Strategic Plan (1PSP). I have used various versions of these tools over the years, but the one that I am using that really works well is the one developed by Verne Harnish (aka The Growth Guy). I use this tool in my Business by Design workshops.

In these workshops, I start with getting the business owners to reaffirm why they went into business in the first place, determining what is possible and what success for their business looks like. The idea is for them to get as clear a picture as possible and then work on the plan to get from where they are today to achieve that ultimate goal, dream to realisation, sound familiar? A great way to get business owners into this space is to ask them to close their eyes and start to visualise where they would like to see their business in three-to-five years' time. To assist them, I ask them questions like, 'What do the business premises look like?', 'Where is it?', 'Who is in the business?', 'How many people?', 'What do they look like?', 'What is the vibe of the place?', 'How do you feel when you walk in the doors?', etc. The clearer the goal you have, the more possible it is to achieve it.

Let's put this into a more tangible and logical order using the 1PSP. You can see an example of this plan on Verne Harnish's website, gazelles. com (or Google "One Page Strategic Plan". The Gazelles website, at the time of printing of this book, offers a free word document version of the 1PSP.)

The 1PSP is designed to encapsulate your big picture goals on the left-hand side of the page, and as you move to the right it provides detail on the milestones, projects and tasks that will help you achieve those goals.

The big picture concepts cover the Business Vision (Why), Values, Core Competencies, Brand Promise and the BHAG. What is a BHAG? Leadership expert Jim Collins calls this the Big Hairy Audacious Goal (BHAG). What is the biggest goal that you can think of which would prove that you have achieved your ultimate business dream? This may be a monetary goal such as earning $1m per year or a goal such as being recognised as the most respected business in the industry. Whatever your goal, make sure that you can measure it to know how you are progressing towards it and when you have achieved it. For example, having a business that is the most respected in the industry is harder to measure than a $1m profit. However, you can still measure industry distinction through tools like surveys. The trick is to set the goal and work out the measurement tool to establish where you are in achieving that goal.

From what I've seen, progression is the most motivating factor we have. We get a sense of motivation and pride when we know that we are achieving what we set out to do. With some businesses, it's harder to see your achievements on a daily basis. A landscaping job that I had whilst going through Uni highlighted this fact for me. The thing I loved about working in that job was the sense of satisfaction I got at the end of the day. I could actually see what I had achieved. It could be as simple as seeing a trench dug or a rock formation placed or something as aesthetically pleasing as a finished garden. Unfortunately, in my business today, I have many days where I can't see what I achieve. Subconsciously I know that I am making a difference, but the results are not always evident. That's when regular feedback becomes key.

I find that one of the biggest issues for a lot of office workers is that they don't know what they actually achieve in a day. They know that they are busy, but they can't see the benefit of what they have done. This usually leads to job dissatisfaction and unhappiness. The way to avoid this is to reflect and review on a daily basis what has been completed. Then assess what the outcome was compared to what was completed. Looking at the daily outcome can be like seeing the trench dug towards having constructed a beautiful garden, which will be admired and enjoyed by the property owners, which is the ultimate goal. Some days, I still go back and have a look at the gardens that I helped create. Similarly, you and your employees need to somehow see the fruits of the labour.

Motivation is almost always linked to emotion. In business, the goal may be to get the business into a position where it is generating a $1m profit. Whilst having $1m in your business bank account would be a great achievement, it by itself is not the motivation. The motivation is financial security and independence, which provides a choice to do more of what you want.

Some years ago I built a beach house, and when I say 'built', I was the owner builder. Yes, I know you're probably thinking that it must've been a disaster, like most people told me when I started. And those remarks challenged me to prove that I could do it, but they were not my motivating factor. The motivating factors were: first, the sense of achievement of building something—like the feeling of being a land-scape gardener, but tenfold—and second, to provide a house for my family and friends to enjoy. Knowing that my kids would grow up in that house and have years of great times was the ultimate motivation. Love inspired me to complete that job.

I encourage you to think deeper about your goals and aspirations. Drill down on what really motivates you and drives you. If you link the goal to an emotional one, then you have a greater chance of sticking to the plan and achieving it. So what is *your* BHAG?

SUCCESS TIP
Work out what your ultimate goal in business is and the scale of measurement to establish progression.

The ultimate goal provides the motivation to build the infrastructure and the discipline to stay on track. However, the ultimate goal can seem a very long way away during the dark days of business. Remember, there are many phases of business. Some are great, but some are really tough and will test you on every level.

In order to stay on track through the different phases, the 1PSP breaks down the BHAG into milestones. Remember, milestones are like townships on a journey. When you reach your next town, you've achieved a mini win in getting towards your ultimate destination. How do we break this down? First define the Key Performance Indicators (KPI) that must be achieved to reach your ultimate goal. These are very high-level numbers such as revenue, cost of sales, gross profit, net profit, business value, number of customers and number of staff/team members.

If we consider that your BHAG is your ultimate measurable destination, then we need to have a map to establish the path and the milestones to assess progress. The best way to do this is to work backwards from your destination. If we consider your BHAG to be at least five years in the future, we want to establish what your yearly goals are along the way. It is sometimes funny to watch people have minor meltdown when I ask them to define what their business will look like in three-to-five years. I admit that through parts of my journey, I too have struggled with this kind of visualisation. We get lost. That is ok. That is why planning is important. It is understandable why some people struggle with this exercise, particularly when they have not practiced planning in their business.

In the 1PSP we ask for high-level information with respect to this projection. To provide clarity and focus, I ask for revenue or turnover, gross profit, net profit, business value, number of customers and number of team members. Some detail-oriented people will try to work this out via a formula by working forwards from where they are. Whilst this will be necessary, it is not what I want them to do yet. I still want them to dream a bit about what they would like to have as their future reality, regardless of whether they can achieve it. If people work the other way around initially, often it limits them as to whether they can achieve their ultimate goal. Once again, like many business owners, I have fallen into this trap. Success largely depends on your confidence in believing that your dream is achievable.

I also ask business owners to visualise what types of customers they would like to work with from the perspective of size, products/services they will purchase, frequency of purchase and culture. We sometimes overlook the importance of cultural fit when it comes to defining our ideal customers if we get caught up with the metrics. I have heard partners in other accounting firms joke about having a better business if they did not have customers or staff. Clearly they never understood the beauty of customer and staff cultures mixed right.

Unless you define what you really want, you will struggle to achieve it. Once we have defined where we would like to be in three-to-five years, we then need to start to get real about how possible it is by working forwards from today. We do this by setting a budget for the next twelve months. Once again, from a strategic perspective, we focus on specific KPIs that are relevant to drive the business. Using the budgeting tools that we have learnt in previous chapters, we define what is possible for the next twelve months from a revenue/profit perspective and the key metrics to achieve this from a sales and marketing and a resources perspective.

If in five years' time we want to have a business turning over $10m to which we need 1,000 customers and fifty staff, then we need to know that we can build the customer base to 300 and have a turnover of $3m and staff of fifteen by the end of the forecasted twelve-month period. At this stage of analysis, we see two things happen: some adjust their 3-5 year projections up or down, and some are chuffed to think that they have a realistic goal that they can achieve, albeit a stretch.

Once we establish the key drivers required to achieve our twelve-month goal, we need to set appropriate projects to ensure that we achieve these, because activities drive results. For example, if one of your key drivers is gaining new customers, then your project should be marketing or sales-oriented tasks to ensure that you meet your growth targets. If another of your key drivers is minimising expenses, a review of your resourcing efficiency may be the project, with the tasks being completing an analysis to determine how to measure people's efficiency, setting tasks and KPIs and then keeping your team accountable to these.

The older we get, the more we feel that time flies. However, a year is a very long time in the business world, so we need to break down yearly goals into quarterly and monthly goals. Once again, this is important for the purpose of taking it one step at a time to ensure that you are keeping on track with the road signs. Yearly KPIs must be broken down into quarterly and monthly KPIs, and yearly projects should be broken down into quarterly and monthly tasks.

The last thing that the 1PSP does is assist in team engagement and alignment through establishing themes. What is a theme, I hear you ask? A theme is an overarching idea for your company culture that is established to focus everyone's energy and attention on the most significant performance or result affecting the revenue, cash, profit or productivity of the business. The best way to ensure that a project is completed as fast as possible with the best outcome is to get your team engaged so that they take ownership of the project. Themes help make that possible.

Our business used a theme to create team engagement and buy in, thus fixing the problem we had, using the example around payment terms in Chapter 6. Since we are an accounting firm, we are a service-based business. As a service-based business, we will complete work for customers and then invoice them once completed. We had a goal to shorten the time it took us to complete tasks, because the longer it takes to complete tasks, the longer it takes to invoice and then ultimately to be paid. At a certain period in our business, this process was really lagging, and it brought the whole business down. We could tell because we measured the work in progress (WIP) days and average debtor days (how long it took to get paid from the time we invoiced). It was taking us on average 113 days to get paid from starting the work, creating what we referred to as 'lock up days'.

We changed a number of processes to ensure that we got paid sooner, like providing discounts for upfront payment, and this shortened our average lock up quite considerably. But we still had to create team buy-in to become even more efficient. So we created a theme called

'WIP It'. Now anyone who's lived through the '80s will have already started singing the song in their head by Devo, 'Whip It'. Devo was a crazy band in the '80s that had a couple of hits. They dressed up in futuristic clothes and wore what looked like upside down plant pots on their heads. One day I took it upon myself to come into the office with an upside down plant pot on my head, carrying a stockman's whip in my hand and blasting the Devo song 'Whip It' from a stereo. Now the team knows that I can be unusual but this made them sit up and take note. Once I explained it was all about the theme, they just laughed. Now that I had their attention, I explained our company's new theme about reducing 'lock up days'. I also provided them with a scoreboard, measurement and incentive. If you want your team to be fully engaged, you need to provide a reward for achievement. We had four levels of measurement—so clear KPIs and four levels of reward. The four levels of KPIs and measurement were as follows:

1. Revenue for the Quarter
2. WIP Days
3. Debtor Days
4. Write-Offs

We set a target for each to be achieved over the next 90-day period. Then we set an incentive for achieving levels 1, 2, 3 and all 4. If they achieved all four, the incentive was that we would take the whole team out for lunch and close the office for the afternoon so they could have the rest of the day off to enjoy themselves. They did achieve all four KPIs, so we did take them out to lunch and close the office. Now I would have thought that after lunch they would have gone and spent some time doing things for themselves, but to my delight they all stayed together and spent the rest of the day and night into the wee hours of the morning in bars and clubs. Now we don't condone drinking; however, we respect that all of our team are mature adults that make good choices so we never have to worry about their behaviour or actions.

The power of the theme was the constant visual presence to remind them of their focus for the quarter. We put posters up and we also had a whiteboard with the KPIs and a meter on how we were progressing to the goal. Everyone was really engaged and worked hard for the result. The really cool part of this for my business was that in three months we wiped out needing our overdraft facility that we had consistently used for five years. How awesome is that!

Can you see that the 1PSP really does connect large concept-related goals to day-to-day tasks and goals? I highly recommend that you use this tool for your business, as it is one of the most powerful tools that I use for my own business and my customers' businesses. This tool helps to push through the different business phases.

Getting back to the phases of business, I could simplify a business down further into two kinds. A business that is reliant upon its owners and a business that is not reliant upon its owners. The true definition of a business from my perspective is one that has a life of its own. To have a life of its own means that there is no reliance or connection with any one individual person. No one person, customer or supplier can devastate the business. Most businesses that start out are heavily reliant upon the business owners for its survival. So if you took the business owner out of the business, the business would die. Take steps to allow your business grow beyond that stage. The next phase to this would be if you build the business to a point where it is no longer reliant on its business owners to survive; it maintains itself. The final phase where a business has a life of its own and is worth the most amount of value is when the business flourishes without the business owner being involved in the business. So the 1PSP assists you in pushing the business through each phase to get to the ultimate goal of creating a business that has a life of its own.

Now that you've charted the map, you need to keep your business on the right track. This is where building in business disciplines comes in. As outlined in Chapter 2, small business can look to large business for clues on how to be successful. One of the key elements of a large business is the structure. Having a board of directors and holding a board meeting regularly is one of the best ways of setting the strategy and holding everyone accountable to the strategy. I lead board meetings with my business customers monthly to ensure that we cover the following:

- Financial Information
- Sales and Marketing
- Human Resources
- Opportunities
- Threats
- Project Accountability
- A health check on how the business owners feel

We record the meeting with minutes and action items to keep the business owners on track with the projects, goals and actions. Some use the 1PSP, and others use different tools. I am not fussed on what tools that you use as long as each of the above topics are covered.

Building this type of infrastructure and discipline on its own actually adds capital value to the business. Prospective buyers will take note and pay a higher price for that value.

> **SUCCESS TIP**
> Identify what phase of business you are in, and develop a strategic map to determine the tasks to achieve the ultimate goal in your business.

Chapter 10

WHAT ARE WE GOING TO DO NOW THAT WE ARE CLOSE TO OUR DESTINATION?

Succession Planning and Beyond

You have finally built your business into what you have always dreamed. It now has a life of its own, and you are ready to make decisions for the future. Like we've already discussed, building your business so it is a saleable commodity does not necessarily mean that you must sell it. From my perspective, it gives you a choice. A choice to stay working either in or on your business, depending on what makes your heart sing. Alternatively, if you are ready to pass it on to someone else, it's time to consider your options for exiting the business. The fancy business term for this phase is 'succession planning'.

The first nine chapters of this book are all about building your business and maximising its value. Remember, the two key elements in building business wealth is increasing the profit and reducing the risk of not achieving the profits in future years, which are the fundamental elements of the business valuation calculation method. Now it's time to realise all the blood, sweat and tears that went into building such an established and valuable asset.

What are your options when it comes to succession planning and determining your ultimate exit from the business? A number of different factors can help you determine the right path for succession planning. Some owners want to maximise the sale price as much as possible before moving on. Others may be motivated by selling to a bigger competitor in order to take the business to another level—one which they may or may not be a part of. Some want to pass the business on to their children to provide them with the opportunity to achieve their own dreams and aspirations. Another possible motivator is to pass the business on to someone who will care for it as much as the owner has, so the legacy can continue on. As you can see, price is not always the only factor to consider when determining the appropriate option for succession planning.

Let's briefly explore some options and consider what's possible.

Trade Sale

A trade sale is when you sell to another business. This may be to a different business for different reasons. A competitor may want to buy your business to grow their business and reduce the competition. The merger process between two similar companies will, hopefully, be smooth as it should be a 'plug and play acquisition'. This sale may command a very high price because your business will be valuable to them. It also means that there can be an immediate extra benefit through what is known as economies of scale. Economies of scale mean that there can be a cost saving due to the increase in size. For example, when two businesses come together, you generally can reduce the team required without compromising the service levels because there is a doubling of resources. The main example that comes to mind is administrative positions; these often become redundant when two businesses come together. There may be other cost savings that occur when two businesses come together which will automatically increase profits.

Another option for a trade sale is that you may be a target for a similar business that is not in your geographic location but wants to be in your location. Rather than set up a competitor business in your location, it is faster and possibly cheaper to buy an existing business in a location that is already established. Once again, the price that a like business will pay to get into your location will be reasonably high. For example, one of my customers was recently purchased for around $10m for the purpose of heading up the Asia Pacific location of the purchaser's business.

Another option is a business that has complementary products, or the same customers, that wants to expand its product or service range. This is known as a vertical integration acquisition. The amount that a business is prepared to pay for this type of value is quite high, because they can use your products to sell to their customers, and they can use your database to sell their products. It is a bit of a double whammy benefit.

I was involved in a sale for one of my customers that sold to a buyer for this reason. Based on the fact that they established a very impressive business, the buyer paid a $4m premium to be able to sell the vendor's business product to their customers and establish the purchaser's business into the vendor's geographic location. This represented a 28% premium.

Finally, a large business may acquire smaller businesses as a roll up strategy or a consolidation of the industry for the benefit of economies of scale, distribution of product and services and minimisation of competitors. This happens in many industries, especially in the accounting industry.

Initial Public Offering (IPO)

An initial public offering (IPO) is also known as a stock market launch, which is a public offering where shares in a company are sold to the general public on the stock market. A private company will transform into a public company through this process.

I have been fortunate to go through this process with a customer. My accounting firm and I were engaged as the virtual CFO for the two years running up to the company wanting to be listed on the stock exchange. During the process, I was on the due diligence committee. A due diligence committee is formed when a business prepares for an IPO to ensure that the business has all of its ducks in a row, so to speak. Most advisors never get the chance to go through this process, so for me it was certainly a highlight in my career.

IPOs are most often used by companies to raise expansion capital. A company selling ordinary shares is not required to repay the capital to its public investors. After the IPO, when shares trade freely in the open market, money passes between public investors. Although an IPO offers many advantages, there are also significant disadvantages. Chief among these are the costs associated with the process and the requirement to disclose certain information that could prove helpful to competitors or create difficulties with vendors. Details of the proposed offering are disclosed to potential purchasers in the form of a lengthy document known as a prospectus. Most businesses undertaking an IPO do so with the assistance of an investment banking firm acting in the capacity of an underwriter. Underwriters provide a valuable service, which includes help with correctly assessing the value of shares (share price) and establishing a public market for shares (initial sale).

This is also a costly exercise; you don't get much change out of $100,000 to complete this process. The process generally takes six months; however, the one that I was involved in took three months due to the time pressure the company was under. There was a window of opportunity for being listed that they wanted to take advantage of it. Whilst it was a successful listing, I would not recommend that you rush the process. Shortening the period puts an enormous pressure on the board, executive and the advisors assisting the process. It can also lead to errors.

There are two main benefits for the business and its owners to be listed on the stock exchange. First, it raises capital for the business to expand the operations and second, it provides a market to sell the ownership in the business to the existing shareholders either partially or completely. In nearly all situations the original shareholders that own the business prior to the listing will be in escrow. This means that they cannot be traded for a period of time. This can be anywhere from six months to six years and potentially beyond.

Generation Change

Some business owners are driven to pass their business on to their children. There are many examples of generational businesses that pass from generation to generation. Whilst this has a feel-good factor, multi-generation businesses are laced with many problems that are not present in non-family businesses. This is largely due to the emotional foundation upon which the families operate, which sometimes is counterproductive to making commercial decisions. Successful family businesses operate in a very commercial decision-making environment.

Have you ever heard the statement that 'the first generation creates it, the second generation capitalises on it and the third generation spends it and loses it'? This has happened countless times, especially in younger countries. For example, in Australia many immigrants came to the country and started businesses. These businesses became multi-generational and followed a similar path. If you want your businesses to go down this path, make sure that you read the stories of multi-generational businesses to learn from their mistakes to ensure that you do not make the same mistakes. It is so important to do this as the mistakes are generally repeated again and again by different businesses—simply driven by the fact that family is involved and emotions direct business decisions rather than commerce.

Another issue with generation changes is that the real value of the business may never be realised as the desire to provide the next generation with a start in life takes precedence over the business's best interests.

Succession Planning Summary

There have been many books written on succession planning, so I am not going to elaborate further on the different options and the advantages and disadvantages of each. But now you have a taste for the different options available for your business in the future.

SUCCESS TIP
When you start out in business, it is good to know what you want to achieve as a final exit. Start with the end in mind. This provides significant vision and focus, giving you a greater chance of achieving it.

I read an interesting article in *The Australian*, by Bernard Salt, 13 April 2017, which stated that there are approximately 2.12 million small businesses in Australia out of 2.17 million total businesses. (Small businesses are defined as companies with nineteen employees or fewer.) This statistic suggests that there is a strong opportunity for small business owners to be able to realise their business value in the future. As Salt quotes in this article, 'We are a nation of small businesses.'

At the end of most of the workshop sessions that I run, I end with a PowerPoint slide, which says: 'We all know what we have to do. The key to success is IMPLEMENTATION.'

There is nothing new in the world of business strategy. Success is all about how you package and then implement your plans. So many times I hear business owners say, 'I know all of this!'— which may be true. So if you know it, are you doing it? There are just two answers to this question: a list of excuses or a decision to change and get things done. You just need to ask yourself, how hungry are you to achieve your dream?

So, how about it? What will you do to achieve your dream? Set this book down and get started!

About the Author

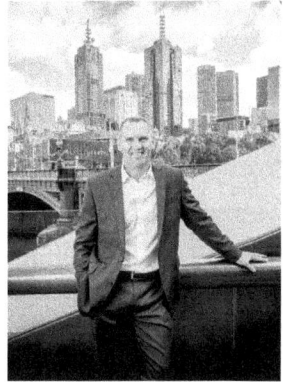

Knowing why you do something is an extremely powerful motivator. The why is the purpose. This is the driving force Matt Murphy uses to continue the growth and success of the accounting, wealth management and capital advisory firm Prime Financial Group.

In his own words, 'My why is to inspire business owners to achieve *their* reason why they went into business in the first place. Business owners are courageous; they have the guts to have a go. Yet unless they're "on purpose", their road to success will be harder than it needs to be.'

At 32, after resigning from being a partner of an accounting firm and with several years working in tax with the Australian Tax Office and in private practice, Matt Murphy did some soul-searching—a summer holiday spent building sandcastles with his son left him pondering what he could build. He realised that he loved business and wanted to build something special to truly support Australian entrepreneurial innovation businesses. Matt assessed the accounting firm market from sole practitioner to Big 4 firms to find a firm with a similar drive and passion.

Matt, now 47, joined accounting firm MPR Group based in Melbourne's bustling Southbank. He came across Marc (Peskett, one of the MPR founders) through a recruiter. Marc's vision of serving clients aligned with the way Matt believed they needed to be looked after. It was about supporting a business in the realisation of their dreams by providing proactive advice rather than simply filling out their tax return or making sure they were compliant from a tax perspective.

Peskett and two others started MPR in 2000 with the vision of supporting entrepreneurial, fast-growing innovative companies – and Matt loved that. MPR provided a full range of accounting, taxation and business advisory services to businesses in every stage and every phase of business. MPR also supported venture capitalists (VC) providing their services to the VC backed innovation lead companies.

Initially, Matt took on numerous roles for the clients of MPR such as Virtual CFO, Company Secretary, Board and CEO Advisor and Business Owner Mentor. 'These companies were crying out for a safe pair of hands they could trust. They needed a combination of strategic thinking and financial information.'

Whilst MPR achieved significant success for its client and in its own right, Matt always had a desire to grow the business beyond Melbourne and offer capital to Australian entrepreneurial innovation-led businesses. A chance meeting with Prime Financial Group Managing Director/CEO Simon Madder through a primary school friend of his wife's who knew of Madder, assisted with the fulfilment of this desire.

Based on the strategic alignment of Prime and MPR's vision, Prime took a 40% stake in MPR in December 2015. That was increased to 93% in August 2016 and 100% in February of this year.

With the recent merger with ASX-listed Prime Financial Group continues the evolution for MPR. Simon and Matt have a very similar philosophy. The fact Prime provides wealth management and capital to clients complements their businesses perfectly. These additional services give customers an integrated end-to-end service that is unique to the Australian market.

This is where Matt gets excited, he really does love helping businesses to succeed.

In Matt's own words, 'Core to our philosophy is to support the business owners' journey. Based on experience, we understand that people who become business owners have a 'why' that includes any or all of the following: they're seeking financial independence (or security), they want to satisfy an entrepreneurial urge, achieve work/life balance, feel that they have some form of control over their destiny and leave a legacy for their family and community.'

'Helping business people realise their dream is amazingly satisfying. Many SMEs fail because they don't have the right infrastructure, discipline and accountability in place. A lot of it comes back to having the right information available to make strategic decisions about where your business is going or needs to go. This underpins the service offering of our firm.'

'If I think about an analogy, it is all about high performance. Our goal is to provide business leaders with the same support that an elite athlete gets, so they can perform at their best.'

Matt performs many advisory roles and works closely with his clients, so close that when one of his clients (innovative health technology company d3 Medicines) was asked to speak at the United Nations in New York, they asked Matt to attend with them.

'Every service that we offer to our clients was created from a need. Businesses require many things to be successful. Fundamental to the success of a growing entrepreneurial business or a start-up is getting the funding right. This is why we offer our clients the support to access government funding programs to do just that.'

Two very effective government funding programs are the Research and Development (R&D) Tax Incentive and the Export Market Development Grant (EMDG). These programs have supported Australian business to achieve success. Matt is proud to say that three of the largest value realisations for Australian Biotechnology based businesses accessing these programs were Prime's clients.

In business change is happening at light speed. R&D of products and services is now paramount to ensure that businesses remain in business. Identifying and developing the right technology is the key for innovation.

'We are extremely excited about the future and how we can continue to support Australian entrepreneurial innovation-led businesses and their owners to ensure that Australia continues to enjoy its status of the "lucky country" and competes on the world stage.'

Bibliography

Author	Books	Bibliography
Jay Abraham	Getting Everything You Can Out of All You've Got	Abraham, Jay. *Getting Everything You Can Out of All You've Got: 21 Ways You Can Out-Think, Out-Perform, and Out-Earn the Competition*. St. Martin's Press, 2001.
Ronald J. Baker	Measure What Matters To Customers	Baker, Ronald J. *Measure What Matters to Customers: Using Key Predictive Indicators (KPIs)*. John Wiley & Sons, Inc., 2006.
	The Firm of the Future	Dunn, Paul and Ronald J. Baker. *The Firm of the Future*. John Wiley & Sons, Inc., 2003.
	Implementing Value Pricing	Baker, Ronald J. *Implementing Value Pricing: A Radical Business Model for Professional Firms*. John Wiley & Sons, Inc., 2010.
Richard Branson	Losing My Virginity	Branson, Richard. *Losing My Virginity*. Random House, Inc., 2011.
Dale Carnegie	How to Win Friends & Influence People	Carnegie, Dale. *How to Win Friends and Influence People*. Simon and Schuster, 1936.
Gary Chapman	The 5 Love Languages	Chapman, Gary. *5 Love Languages: The Secret to Love That Lasts*. Moody Press, U.S., 2014.
Clayton M. Christensen	The Innovator's Dilemma	Christensen, Clayton M. *The Innovator's Dilemma: When New Technologies Cause Great Firms to Fail*. Harvard Business Press, 1997.

Author	Books	Bibliography
Jim Collins	Good to Great	Collins, Jim. *Good to Great: Why Some Companies Make the Leap ... And Others Don't.* Illustrated. HarperCollins, 2001.
Stephen R. Covey	The 7 Habits of Highly Effective People	Covey, Stephen R. *The 7 Habits of Highly Effective People.* Free Press, 1989.
Mihaly Csikszentmihalyi	Flow	Csikszentmihalyi, Mihaly. *Flow.* HarperCollins, 2008.
His Holiness Dalai Lama and Howard C. Cutler. M.D.	The Art of Happiness	Dalai Lama, His Holiness and Cutler, Howard C. *The Art of Happiness: A Handbook for Living.* Penguin Putnam Inc., 1998.
Peter F. Drucker	The Essential Drucker	Drucker, Peter F. *The Essential Drucker.* HarperCollins, 2001.
Timothy Ferriss	The 4-Hour Workweek	Ferriss, Timothy. *The 4-Hour Workweek.* Expanded and Updated. Crown Publishing Group, 2009.
Adam Fraser	The Third Space: Using Life's Little Transitions to Find Balance and Happiness	Fraser, Adam. *The Third Space: Using Life's Little Transitions to Find Balance and Happiness.* Random House Australia, 2012.
Thomas L. Friedman	The World Is Flat	Friedman, Thomas L. *The World Is Flat [Further Updated and Expanded; Release 3.0]: A Brief History of the Twenty-first Century,* Farrar, Strauss and Giroux, 2007.
Rudolph W. Giuliani and Ken Kurson	Leadership	Giuliani, Rudolph W. and Kurson, Ken. *Leadership.* Diane Pub Co, 2002.
Malcolm Gladwell	Outliers	Gladwell, Malcolm. *Outliers.* Little, Brown and Company, 2008.

Author	Books	Bibliography
Daniel Goleman	Emotional Intelligence: Why It Can Matter More Than IQ	Goleman, Daniel. *Emotional Intelligence: Why It Can Matter More Than IQ*. Bantam Books, 1997.
Verne Harnish	Mastering the Rockefeller Habits	Harnish, Verne. *Mastering the Rockefeller Habits: What You Must Do to Increase the Value of Your GrowingFirm*. Select Books Incorporated, 2002.
Terri Irwin	My Steve	Irwin, Terri. *My Steve*. Simon & Schuster, 2007.
James Kerr	Legacy	Kerr, James. *Legacy: What the All Blacks Can Teach Us About the Business of Life*. Little, Brown Book Group, 2013.
David Maister	Managing the Professional Service Firm	Maister, David. *Managing The Professional Service Firm*. Simon and Schuster, 2012.
	The Trusted Advisor	Maister, David. *The Trusted Advisor*. Simon and Schuster, 2012.
	Practice What You Preach	Maister, David. *Practice What You Preach: What Managers Must Do to Create High Achievement Culture*. Simon and Schuster, 2012.
	True Professionalism	Maister, David. *True Professionalism: The Courage to Care about Your People, Your Clients, and Your Career*. Simon and Schuster, 2012.
Alex Malley	The Naked CEO	Malley, Alex. *The Naked CEO: The Truth You Need to Build a Big Life*. John Wiley & Sons Australia Ltd, 2014.
John C. Maxwell	The 21 Irrefutable Laws of Leadership	Maxwell, John C. *The 21 Irrefutable Laws of Leadership*. Thomas Nelson Publishers, 2007.

Author	Books	Bibliography
NLP Comprehensive	NLP: The New Technology of Achievement	NLP Comprehensive. *NLP: The New Technology of Achievement.* William Morrow Paperbacks, 2011.
Daniel H. Pink	Drive	Pink, Daniel H. *Drive: The Surprising Truth About What Motivates Us.* Canongate Books, 2010.
Daniel Priestley	Oversubscribed: How to Get People Lining Up to Do Business with You	Priestley, Daniel. *Oversubscribed: How to Get People Lining Up to Do Business with You.* Capstone, 2015.
Barry Schwartz	The Paradox of Choice: Why More Is Less	Schwartz, Barry. *The Paradox of Choice: Why More Is Less.* Ecco, 2016.
Martin Seligman	Learned Optimism	Seligman, Martin. *Learned Optimism.* Random House Australia, 2011.
	Authentic Happiness: Using the New Positive Psychology to Realize Your Potential for Lasting Fulfillment	Seligman, Martin. *Authentic Happiness: Using the New Positive Psychology to Realize Your Potential for Lasting Fulfillment.* Simon and Schuster, 2002.
Dr. Seuss	Oh, the Places You'll Go	Dr. Seuss and Carter, David. *Oh, the Places You'll Go.* Random House, 1990.
Peter Sheahan	Flip	Sheahan, Peter. *Flip: How Counter-Intuitive Thinking is Changing Everything.* HarperCollins, 2009.

Author	Books	Bibliography
Simon Sinek	Start With Why	Sinek, Simon. *Start With Why: How Great Leaders Inspire Everyone to Take Action.* Illustrated, reprint. Portfolio/ Penguin, 2011.
Amanda Stevens	Turning Customers Into Advocates: 10 Steps to Creating Raving Fans for Any Business	Stevens, Amanda. *Turning Customers Into Advocates: 10 Steps to Creating Raving Fans for Any Business.* Amanda Stevens Pty Ltd, 2016.

Connect with Matt on social media

@MattMurphyMPR

Matthew Murphy

matthewm.mpr

mattm@primefinancial.com.au

www.ingramcontent.com/pod-product-compliance
Lightning Source LLC
Chambersburg PA
CBHW060514090426
42735CB00011B/2211